Jesus Wears Socks *with* Sandals

41 STORIES
of Humanity Being Ridiculously Lovable

S. James Meyer

TWENTY-THIRD
PUBLICATIONS
twentythirdpublications.com

Twenty-Third Publications
One Montauk Avenue, Suite 200
New London, CT 06320
(860) 437-3012 or (800) 321-0411
www.twentythirdpublications.com

Cover photo: ©Shutterstock / Fred van Diem

ISBN: 978-1-62785-558-7
Printed in the U.S.A.

A division of Bayard, Inc.

Wow. Just wow! Michelle, you didn't know what you were signing up for when you said "I do" thirty-three years ago. Thank you for your blind faith. Or your naivete. But certainly for your support. People who know me well know what you have to deal with. All are impressed and amazed by your character, strength, and perseverance. Rightly so.

Adam, Alex, and Jacob, you had no choice in this arrangement. Well, maybe you did on a spiritual plane. We really don't know. You were born into this. Each of you arrived as an open window to the wisdom of the ages, and you've generously let the light shine through. I've learned so much from you. Go figure.

Thank you for allowing me to tag along as you've encountered life's story and for giving my own story added shape and depth in the process.

Table of Contents

Before You Even Get Started

Alex snuck quietly into the church and removed the cover from the grand piano. He had been eyeing up the instrument since it had been installed five years prior. Very few people in the parish, certainly none of the staff or volunteers who were mingling about that afternoon, knew he had been taking lessons for eleven years. Knowing him only as the kid who sat on the sanctuary steps during Mass as a toddler, and the always-smiling server who could be counted on week in and week out throughout his youth, they had no idea what a gifted musician he had become. Odd how we do that to each other, isn't it? How we miss each other's gifts because we've already defined them?

In the dark corner of the church, Alex opened the piano's top with the confidence of someone who had done it a hundred times before. He stretched his long fingers and played a few soft scales. Once comfortable with the instrument, he began playing a rich, embodied "Clair de Lune" that infused the entire church with fresh breath. Time paused to create space for unexpected music. Father Paul emerged from his office to follow the sound, with four staff members and three volunteers trailing behind. They stood in the back of the church, unable to make out the shadow behind the piano. When he finished, they expressed appreciation with a smattering of applause.

Alex immediately uncorked the real reason he came to the church that afternoon. Pushing back the bench and standing at the keys, he ripped into a perfect rendition of Billy Joel's "Piano Man." A few among the gathered assembly shifted uncomfortably. Was this appropriate in a church? They weren't quite sure how to respond. Standing in an entrance on the other side, I held my breath, both proud of and nervous for my son.

Father Paul knew exactly what to do. "Bravo!" he shouted across the nave. "Bravo!" He moved closer to see the identity of the pianist. "Alex? Is that you, Alex? I had no idea you were so gifted! Thank you for sharing that with us!"

That's the closest Alex ever got to rebelling against the Church. Until he quietly left.

Alex is a bright guy. I'm not talking about your garden-variety-advanced-algebra brightness. Sure, he might not know how to fix the lawnmower. Come to think of it, I'm not sure he knows how to use the lawnmower. Maybe that's not fair. Maybe. But intellectually he breathes rare air. He understands things like binary asteroids and how to calculate the orbital trajectory of Jupiter's moons. I don't know why anyone would need to know that, but he does.

He also understands people. I mean, he really gets them. Alex has amazing social intelligence, which strikes me as a bit surprising for a space geek whose leading passions, even as an adult, are Lego and *Star Wars*. Music, science, humanity—it all comes naturally to Alex. But the one thing Alex doesn't understand in spite of an immersive upbringing is organized religion. As Alex went through high school and college, he still loved the parish and loved the people, but he grew increasingly disenchanted with organized religion in general, which he accused of hypocrisy and exclusion. I tried reframing hypocrisy as the human condition and exclusion as tribalism, but Alex wouldn't bite.

When I shared the title of this book with him, I was shocked at how vehemently he objected. I had thought his passions for faith had waned to nary a whisper. Boy, was I wrong! "Just stop," he said. "Before you even get started, just stop. Jesus is *not* a dweeb!" The more he talked, the more animated he became. He was adamant about protecting the image and reputation of his very good friend, Jesus.

"That's the point," I countered. "Jesus seeks to live, breathe, work through, and be present in every person, no exceptions." I added the *no exceptions* part to appeal to his millennial sense of radical inclusion. It did get him to pause. For a moment.

"But he would not wear socks with sandals," he insisted.

I wrote the stories in this book to emphasize how human Jesus is and how sacred humans are. I fear we are losing connection with both sides of that equation. Religion doesn't make sense to a lot of people anymore because we've created this false divide between Christ and humanity, seeing them as separate rather than as a common union—many parts, one body.

The stories in this book are divided into sections because it helps the content seem organized and the reader feel oriented. In truth, life has a way of unfolding both sequentially and randomly, often at the same time. It's seldom tidy. Some structure is helpful; much of it is arbitrary. In this book, it's mostly inconsequential. If you're the type of person who sticks to your grocery list, start at the front and read straight through. It'll feel more comfortable for you. If, however, you're more inclined to wander aimlessly and let surprising things fall into your shopping cart, go nuts and approach it like a book of poems you open willy-nilly. There are no rubrics here. Thanks be to God.

Wisdom

Go, Mennonite Guy!

The Mennonite guy has the best tomatoes. Normally, I'm not a big fan of the ol' love apples. Unless I'm squeezing them from a bottle onto a burger or spooning them spiced over pasta, I'm typically not interested. But the optics of the Mennonite guy's tomatoes are irresistible. They are metaphors for something, everything, that is or can be right in the world. My weekly stroll past the stand he tends with his ruddy-cheeked daughters is a favorite Farmers Market ritual for me. These earnest, sincere people with those amazing tomatoes have the power to stop time.

Directly across from the Mennonite guy is a stand run by a throwback hippie couple selling organic vegetables. They are rare gems of a different sort, with an unwavering dedication to ideals long since abandoned by most of their generation. They pay a price for their convictions, however. Their bounty is not as robust as the high-yield farmers. They offer more root vegetables, such as leeks, radishes, and carrots, giving their display a more earthy tone. I love their soft-spoken, gentle conversation and unassuming smiles.

I relish the moment each Saturday morning when I occupy the poetic space between the Mennonite guy and the hippie couple. They come from vastly different worlds yet have so much in common. It's a fascinating human harmony of contrasts and synergies. Both are rooted in bygone eras, clinging religiously to their values and resisting what the world thinks of as progress. Go, Mennonite guy and his ruddy-cheeked daughters! Go, hippie couple! Although I know neither of them, I am so thankful for both of them. Secretly, I envy their convictions and honor their values, even as I choke on the hypocrisy of my own unwillingness to give up ESPN or cheese curds.

These are but two stands in the sea of diversity that has become my local Farmers Market. The rows of white awnings shade a potpourri of humanity created in God's image and likeness: extended Hmong families, Native Americans, Indian immigrants, and Hispanic Americans all peppered among Euro-American old-timers who've farmed in the area for generations.

Flowing shoulder-to-shoulder, a lazy river of folk in all shapes, sizes, ages, and colors meanders from stand to stand. They continuously get in each other's way, clogging arteries with neighborly conversation and tripping over strollers. No one seems to mind. No one is in a hurry as they sip coffee and eat spring rolls. This is the poetry of the Farmers Market. It renews my spirit and inspires my belief in humanity. It also leaves me wondering why we can't live like this all the time. If thousands of people with diverse histories and stories can crowd together each week in a downtown Farmers Market, what stops us from doing so elsewhere and always?

This may be the closest thing I know to actually being church beyond the Church. It's a common humanity, void of pretension, each person created as a unique self-portrait of the Creator, and all gathered by a common need to be nourished. At the end of the day, the Mennonite guy, the hippie couple, and the Catholic deacon-dad standing between them have nothing and every-thing in common. Can we carry the spirit of the Farmers Market beyond the market? If not, the experience has been diminished. Can we carry the spirit of church beyond the Church? If not, the experience has been diminished.

Pollsters and Prophets

The doorbell rang. I took a deep breath and held it a bit before letting it out slowly. Earlier in the day I had spotted a couple of young men in white short-sleeved dress shirts and black ties a few blocks over. They looked like copier repairmen but happier, with more of a sense of purpose. On a Saturday morning, this could only mean one thing—doorbell evangelists hitting the bricks to save souls. I reminded myself to have an open heart. After all, who couldn't use a good soul saving once in a while?

When I answered the door, I was surprised and confused by the sight of a young man wearing jeans and an unbuttoned flannel shirt over a plain black t-shirt. He had not come to recruit me to join him among the chosen who will escape the raging fires of an eternal hell. Not at all. He was taking a survey with just one question. Without glancing at his clipboard, he looked straight at me and asked, "Are you better off today than you were four years ago?" Oh great, I thought, a campaign volunteer disguised as a pollster. I'd rather chew glass for ten minutes. But he was standing on the front step of my home, where two of the house rules are unconditional positive regard and radical hospitality. I would smile warmly and engage.

"Let's see...am I better off?" I repeated his question while looking skyward and stroking my graying beard. "I've learned a lot in the past four years. I've suffered some and grown from it. My spirituality is stronger, so, yes, I am better off."

Silence. He just stood there and looked at me.

Of course, I knew what he had been driving at. It's a question that has been posed every election cycle since Ronald Reagan asked it way back in 1980. Regardless of the incumbent party or the condition of the economy, every challenger asks it with the presumption that we all believe our lives are getting progressively worse and it's an incumbent politician's fault. And now I was being asked it again. Am I better off than I was four years ago? This question has been asked so often over the last forty years that we have come to accept it as a litmus test for deciding how to use our voting power.

As I stood on my doorstep and looked at the perplexed young man, it occurred to me that this question is exactly opposite from the famous John F. Kennedy inaugural quote in 1961: "Ask not what your country can do for you—ask what you can do for your country." In those days, a time many remember with naively romantic nostalgia, we as a culture lived from the inside-out. We were encouraged to ponder what we could each do to serve the greater good of all. But something happened in the twenty years that followed, so that by 1980 we were living from the outside-in, asking ourselves not what we could do for one another in the broader community but rather what the broader community had done for us. Am I better off?

We had transitioned from the servant ethic to the master ethic, from a belief that the community should benefit from me to a belief that I should benefit from the community. It's a transition from a production ethos to a consumer ethos. And not only have we applied it to our politics, but as a culture we have also applied it to our faith.

A while ago when I was visiting with a group of high school students, the issue of Mass attendance came up. "I don't go to church," one of the students offered, "because there's nothing there for me." Others nodded in agreement. "And my parents don't go either," someone else chimed in, "because they don't get anything out of it."

Indeed, the consumer ethic is rooted in at least two generations. As a culture, we seem to have become reticent to invest ourselves in anything that does not promise a direct and immediate personal benefit.

Back in 1961, when Catholics crowded into churches every Sunday morning for a Mass that was offered in Latin via a very low-grade sound system, they thumbed their rosary beads, murmured devotions, and mostly stole glances at their watches. But still they came. Perhaps many were driven by a fear of hell, a sense of Sunday obligation, or a desire to adhere to social expectations, but seeded in those shadowy motivations was a sense of humility, an acknowledgment that my life is but one piece of a larger picture. They came from a culture in which the preferred (if not always practiced) social and moral disposition included a servant ethic. The questions JFK was asking each American to ponder were *What gifts do I have to offer?* not *What are you doing for me?* And *What can I give?* not *What am I getting?*

Faith isn't retail and Christianity isn't Amazon Prime. The gospel makes it pretty clear that true disciples are not bargain hunters, hoping to get something for the lowest possible cost. That's the disposition James and John—two apostles Jesus loved very much—brought to him when they were arguing over who Jesus favored more. They wanted to get something for themselves—a choice seat at a metaphorical banquet table. They were in it for their own benefit. "You don't understand," Jesus tells them. "Can you drink from the cup that I drink? None of this is about serving the self." In fact, Jesus goes on to tell them and us whoever wishes to be great among you will be your servant. Whoever wishes to be first among you will be slave of all. For the Son of Man did not come to be served but to serve (Mt 20:26–28).

This is hard stuff. This Christianity business is tough, and

I sure wish I were a lot better at it. But if we take it seriously, we need to embrace the idea of living from the inside-out. If the litmus test for our lives is *Am I better off?* then we're not getting it at all. It is far better that we ask *Who is better off because of me?*

Loving Nerds on Mondays

In the brilliant 1985 movie *The Breakfast Club*, five high school kids are required to serve detention on Saturday in their large suburban school library. This premise messes up my entire notion of heaven and hell. When I was sixteen, I would have seen the idea of spending an entire Saturday in the library as cruel and eternal punishment, but forty years later the idea strikes me as heavenly bliss. What changed?

Each of the movie's primary characters arrives wearing a mask of superiority. One thinks she is better than the others because she's super popular and comes from a wealthy family. Another because he's a star athlete who works hard in pursuit of goals. The third believes he's better because he's academically gifted and smarter than the rest. The fourth, who society would label a burnout, thinks he's superior because he is more authentic and comes from the real world. He postures himself as cooler, tougher, and having a better grip on the world beyond the falsehoods of high school. And finally, there's an aloof girl who observes everyone from a distance with the superior air of a theater critic. They're thrown together in the library for the day and told they each need to write a paper on the topic "Who am I?"

It's sort of what life as a whole is like when you think about it.

We often put on masks and project images that disguise our true stories and protect our vulnerability, and then we try to figure out who we really are. Such is the human story, from God telling Moses "I am who I am" to Jesus asking his disciples, "Who do people say that I am?" Indeed, who am I? Is this not the question we all pilgrim toward (or intentionally avoid) from the moment we become self-aware until the moment we pass away?

As the day unfolds, these students who started out judging one another grow to realize they're far more alike than different. They open up and share their personal stories, admitting their fears, confronting their insecurities, and exposing their vulnerabilities. Eventually, after shedding their false postures, they discover their suffering and sin are great equalizers. They're really all the same—incomplete, broken, hurting people who want nothing more than to be loved and accepted for who they are behind the masks. A bond of unity forms. Hopefully, that's what we allow our experience around the communion table to do for us.

But then, with the walls they had built around themselves lying in crumbled fragments, one of them asks the million-dollar question of the others: What's going to happen on Monday? Will they carry this experience with them or leave it in the library? Will they dare to walk the high school hallways with their faces exposed, or will they cower behind the social protection of the false images they wear? Will the super popular girl, when she's hanging out by her locker with her friends, say hello to the nerd or the burnout? Do they each believe in their own authenticity? If not, then the experience in the library has been meaningless.

That's the question the gospels dare us to confront. What's going to happen on Monday? We gather in the church, we share our stories, we admit our brokenness, and we enter into holy communion with one another. That's all good and it feels right. But what's going to happen on Monday? Do we leave it in the church, or do we take it into the world? Will we enter Monday with a new sense of unity and community, or will we revert to a paradigm of separateness, individualism, and divisiveness?

At the end of the movie, the five students submit a single essay with a poignant message to the vice principal: *We think you're crazy to make us write an essay telling you who we think we are. You see us as you want to see us, in the simplest terms with the most convenient definitions. But what we found out is that each one of us is a brain and an athlete and a basket case and a princess and a criminal.*

What about us? Do we enter Monday seeing people as we want to see them, in the simplest terms with the most convenient definitions? Do we see people by the labels pinned on them and the masks given to them—sick, wealthy, homeless, gay, poor, successful, Muslim, thin, immigrant, smart, and so on? Eucharist demands that we see others in ourselves and ourselves in all others. There is no rich, poor, male, female, slave, free in Christ. There is only one body of Christ.

Shattered Pearls

Michelle and I were just kids when we moved to Green Bay—in our mid-twenties—and admittedly a little immature. At least I was. Nearly thirty years later, Michelle's still strikingly young and I'm still proudly immature, so some things haven't changed. The move was a tough adjustment, like wearing brand-new shoes on the wrong feet. We felt awkward and uncomfortable. We knew no one in this strange city, we were alone with no family or friends, and we had recently become first-time parents. And, oh yes, it was the dead of winter. And we were broke. So we stayed home a lot, staring at the eggshell walls of a two-bedroom apartment. It was an exciting time in many ways, but an empty time in other ways. We felt lost, a little frightened, and a lot overwhelmed. In retrospect, I don't think it's good for young parents to be alone with no community of family and friends to support them. When such couples move into our workplaces, neighborhoods, and especially our churches, I hope we reach out with support.

Michelle and I tried to put up a good front. Being young, we thought it important to project an image of strong confidence, like we had it all together. Of course, it was all a ruse. As new parents, we had no idea what we were doing; at least I didn't. Michelle had more of an instinct for dealing with sleepless nights, endless crying, and rocket-propelled diaper blowouts. I, on the other hand, found it utterly absurd that God would entrust this child to my parentage.

In our effort to find some sense of connection and community in our new city, we went church shopping, hoping to discover a welcoming parish where we felt like we belonged. Sadly, this was disheartening. In most places, we received cold stares whenever our infant son would fuss. In one case, before Mass even started and while Jacob was actually, thankfully, sleeping, a woman leaned over and without any sort of greeting or welcome offered, "There's a cry room in the back." To me, those words sounded a lot like, "Please take your child and get out of here." We stayed, of course, and I secretly hoped Jacob would wake up, scream, and propel spit-up in her direction. He didn't.

Finally, we stumbled into a church tucked into the woods on the far west side of the city. As soon as we walked in, something felt different. Life! There were children, families, smiles, and laughter. We took a seat buried deep in the congregation. Jacob was about six months old and having a tough, cranky morning. Michelle and I were both frustrated and exhausted, but we did our best to act like our life was under control. Then, as we stood for the creed, Jacob grabbed at Michelle's necklace, gave it a tug, and, snap! Little white fake pearls cascaded onto the floor, bouncing and rolling in all directions. As people and as parents, we felt as broken as that necklace and as lost as those beads scattered in the church.

But something amazing happened. People all around us started picking up the beads. One by one, throughout the rest of the Mass, they handed them back to us. For the first time in all the months since we had moved to Green Bay, we felt the support of a family. We were among friends who understood and helped us pick up the pieces. That was Eucharist—people reaching out and helping one another hold it together.

For us to fully experience that holy communion, we needed to reach the emptiness of that low point. We needed to be broken and scattered on the floor. Blessed are the poor in spirit, for the kingdom of heaven is theirs.

What If the Spirit Doesn't Want Wonton?

The babysitter had been procured. The door closed and latched behind them, and Angela and Brian let out a deep sigh. They paused, listened to the birds, and took a long draw of the early evening sunset. "Free at last, free at last," Brian joked—or half-joked, actually. For nearly a month they had been anticipating this evening, this escape back into the relationship they had known prior to having children. They would go to a grown-up restaurant, the kind that doesn't have crayons on the table, where they would order food requiring forks and knives. It would be just them, only them. They would linger in conversation, maybe cap the evening with a slow walk, and by the time they returned, the children would be sleeping. Hopefully.

As they settled into the car and buckled their seatbelts, both intentionally ignored the empty car seats in back. There was no need to acknowledge them, not tonight. Brian turned to Angela, "It's so quiet."

"Yes," Angela said. "I forgot life could be like this." She leaned over and pecked him on the cheek. Renewal.

He put the car in reverse and let it roll back. "Where would you like to go?"

There was a long pause before she replied, "I don't care. Where would you like to go?"

Another pause, longer than the first. "Really, it doesn't matter to me. Wherever we can relax together. Your choice."

They both rolled their eyes, frustrated with the other for not making the decision easy, but also painfully aware that each is no better. Both wanted the evening to be wonderful; neither wanted to own the responsibility of the decision that would shape it. Finally, Angela said, "Well, I'm not hungry for Chinese."

What just happened?

The famed economic psychologist and Nobel laureate Daniel Kahneman says we do this all the time. We don't like having to think very hard, so when we're faced with a question that makes us think hard, we simply substitute a different question. It's called the substitution heuristic. The question "Where would I like to go for dinner?" would require thinking through a number of different options and evaluating the choices, so instead we substitute a different question, "Am I hungry for Chinese?"

The problem is that we do this with life's big questions, questions we really should think about. For example, the hard question "How can I love and connect with people who are different from me?" is substituted with the much easier question: "Am I a good person?"

These easier questions conveniently let us off the hook with simple, dualistic solutions: yes or no, right or wrong, good or bad. *Yes, I love Jesus. Abortion is wrong. I am a good person. Let's get ice cream.* These are all good answers, correct in their own right, but they are good answers to simple questions. They enable us to waltz through life with a relatively superficial spirituality that is seldom challenged to grow deeper through questions such as *How do I recognize Jesus in others? In what ways do I devalue life? What does it mean to be a good person? Let's get ice cream and talk about it.*

We play this same mind game with ourselves and with others, replacing difficult questions with easy platitudes. *You're either with us or against us.* It makes it easy, but it also creates a polarizing division in our culture. It sets up a forced choice fallacy with only two options and no middle ground. Jesus faced the same thing two thousand years ago. The complex question, "How do we balance the mandates of the law against the teaching of compassion and forgiveness?" was substituted with the simple question, "Should we stone the adulteress? Yes or no?" Jesus, of course, answered the harder question, not the easier one.

Jesus rejected duality, which divided people and pitted them against each other. Instead, he exemplified a better approach, a holistic approach. Like us, he had an imaginative and discerning mind, a compassionate human heart, and a divine soul gifted in wisdom, courage, forgiveness, and fortitude. He lived and loved with all his mind, all his heart, and all his soul. It's the same Trinity into which we were baptized in the name of the Father, and of the Son, and of the Holy Spirit. And each time we make the sign of the cross, touching our minds, which are divine gifts capable of creative and abstract thought, our hearts, which pump the sacred blood of the covenant, and our lungs, which breathe the whispering wind of the Holy Spirit, we recommit ourselves to lives of wholeness, not duality, of communion, not division.

If we want to heal the divisions in our lives, in our families, in our Church, and in our society, we need to do as Jesus did and choose a Trinitarian life over a dualistic life. We need to stop reducing every complex issue to yes or no, right or wrong, good or bad, and instead seek to love wholly with all our mind, all our heart, and all our soul. While duality fosters absolutism, judgmentalism, and conflict, Trinity fosters imagination, engagement, and communion. If we want to heal and be whole, we need to do so with all our mind, heart, and soul, in the name of the Father, and of the Son, and of the Holy Spirit.

The Challenge to Step Up

Buckle up. We're going for a ride, full egghead mode. So take a moment to refresh your coffee, clear the cobwebs, and get ready to rock.

The widely noted and often quoted psychologist/philosopher/

guru Ken Wilber has studied all the -alities and -ologies—spirituality, psychology, anthropology, sociology, theology—and he noticed how all of these studies of the human experience identify various stages of development. Some identify five stages, some seven, and so forth, but when Wilber layered them on top of one another, he noticed a pattern of four foundational stages common to all: egocentrism, ethnocentrism, pluralism, and universalism. OK, those are cognac-sipping words and I come from a beer-drinking world, so allow me to bring it to my own level:

Stage One: Life is about what's best for me.

Stage Two: Life is about what's best for my tribe—us versus them.

Stage Three: Life is about what's best for all tribes—us with them.

Stage Four: Life is about what's best for us—we are all one; there is no *them*.

Now, before we strap up the boots and wade deeper into all this, let me offer a couple of observations about Ken Wilber. First, the dude is one interesting cat. If you ever get a seat next to him at a party, do *not* give it up. He is going to blow your mind. While the rest of us are sorting through life's pieces and trying to make sense of how it all fits together, Ken Wilber somehow sees the completed puzzle and spends his energy breaking it down into pieces the rest of us can understand. It's a gift. Second, he is ridiculously prolific, his books are off-the-charts intense, and he makes me feel like a punk. Seriously, one chapter in any of his books is packed with more thinking than I've done in my entire life. And he writes about everything—psychology, religion, spirituality, mysticism, business, politics, science, sex, ecology—but he writes about all these things as though they are all one thing.

He even has a book called *A Brief History of Everything*, which really is a brief history of everything. It's wild.

In the first stage—egocentrism (think of it as individualism)—we are primarily interested in the self. This is where we all start in life, and it largely defines childhood. Our relationships with other people are utilitarian, focused on how I benefit from the relationship. There is me and everyone else. A lot of Christians stay stuck at this level where the primary motivation is to get a window seat on the glory train called heaven. Look out for number one. I want the biggest cookie.

In the second stage—ethnocentrism (think of it as tribalism)—we are primarily interested in us versus them. We have our tribe and we pledge ourselves to it. Relationships at this stage focus on defining who is in and who is out. Are you with us or against us? Most of us were at this stage of development in high school, where we sported the uniform and colors of our school and fed our pride on a deep disdain for rival schools. Many religions codify and ritualize structure around the tribal stage. There is, admittedly, a real comfort of rooted belonging here, but it ultimately feeds unity on only a small scale while driving divisions on a much grander scale.

The third stage—pluralism—is a subtle but giant leap. Instead of seeing the world as us versus them, we see it as us *with* them. We have our beliefs, language, practices, and so forth, and they have theirs, but we don't have to fight over it. In fact, we can share and maybe learn from each other. This is good Samaritan, woman at the well kind of stuff. I may be a Cheesehead Packers fan, but some of my best friends are skol-slinging Vikings fans. I don't understand it and I cannot relate, but I love them just the same. And I pray for them. Oh, how I pray for them.

Wilber estimates that half the world still hasn't grown past the second stage, tribalism/ethnocentrism, while half has moved on to the third stage, pluralism, and this is what is causing so much conflict and stress in our world right now. I think it's fair to say this tension is fueling America's immigration debate and the resurgence of racism. Is it us versus them or us *with* them?

Now, whatever stage you're at, you think you've arrived at the final stage. You think you have it figured out, and all your thoughts and opinions about the world make sense from that construct. How can anyone not see it? But you don't realize there is more growth ahead. So someone at stage two cannot understand someone at stage three. It's so obvious to them that these other people with their weird languages and practices are a threat to our tribe. And the people who have moved on to stage three are saying, "They're not a threat. They're interesting and, actually, we have a lot in common with them. Can't you see it?" But no, they can't.

This brings us to stage four—universalism. This is clearly where Jesus is, and it's where he invites us to join him. At stage four, there is no *us* and *them*; there is only us—the children of God. Though we are many parts, we are all one body—one body of Christ. Thus, Paul writes to Timothy, "the word of God is not chained." It frees us to transcend the confines of walls and borders so we can enter with Jesus into this one universal body, this kingdom of God.

This idea plays out in the gospel where a man with two layers of separation—he's a leper and he's a Samaritan—is the only man who returns to connect with Jesus. The point is simple: no one is too far removed from the body of Christ. No one. But we have to be willing to let go of the petty, circumstantial, and often man-made contrivances that separate us. What holds us back?

Understanding

God Grants Do-Overs

One of the best things about being a kid is that you get do-overs. I remember getting nearly all the questions wrong on a fourth-grade social studies quiz because I accidentally skipped over question number three, so all the rest of my answers were one spot off on the answer sheet. I had unwittingly identified the Mississippi River as the Great Potato Famine, which, for the record, is arguably not incorrect. There are no potatoes growing in the Mississippi. Mrs. Caskey took me aside and said, "I see what happened. You can retake the quiz during recess if you want." Just like that. No big deal. No lawsuits or attorneys. Just a simple do-over.

We don't get do-overs very often as adults. Try it if you ever get nabbed for driving 78 in a 65. Argue with the officer for a while and then ask for a do-over. Offer to turn around, go back a mile or two and then drive past his radar a second time. See what it gets you. We typically don't give one another a lot of do-overs as grown-ups.

"Mr. Johnson, your firm really messed up our tax returns. We're taking our business elsewhere."

"It was an innocent mistake, Ms. Uhura. I accidentally used tax tables from 1973."

"But now I have to sell my dental work to pay the interest and penalties."

"Can I have a do-over?"

While we don't grant each other a lot of do-overs, God does. The ancient narrative of the Babylonian invasion, exile, and return is the story of a great big do-over. After escaping Egypt and wandering through the desert for a couple of generations, the Hebrews finally had the life they always dreamed of in a land flowing with milk and honey, great schools, and a Starbucks on every corner. Life was good. Maybe too good. People lost perspective. When every box of Cracker Jacks contains a prize, it's human nature to feel a little cheated when you get the cheesy rub-on tattoos while someone else gets the cool magnifying glass. So it was for the Jews. Comfort without gratitude leads to entitlement and self-satisfaction. Yahweh became an afterthought. While they were preoccupied with season five of *The Bachelorishah*, the Babylonians invaded, removed them from this Promised Land, and marched them into exile in Babylon. All was lost. But then God sent the Persian King Cyrus to conquer the Babylonians and allow the Jews to return to Jerusalem. Darkness was lifted. There was a party in the street with live music, fireworks, and all-beef hot dogs. God had granted a do-over!

From a certain Christian point of view, the entire gospel documents a great do-over of sorts. For thousands of years, God had been inviting humanity to step up and enter fully into union, but we kept going through the motions without truly opening our hearts. So finally God says, "Do over! If you won't come to me, I'll come to you." And it's all summed up in that simple line, "God so loved the world that he gave his only son."

But do-overs work only if we accept them. We have to be willing to stop fighting, to stop insisting we're right, to skip a recess, and to try again. Not everyone accepted Jesus or his message. Even today, even with the best intentions, we ourselves can be skeptical. We hear the offer to enter new light, but still we cling to the darkness. How much of our spiritual energy do we channel toward the shadows of our pettiness rather than the light of our potential? How much of our prayer is invested in our problems rather than our promise?

As a world community, we miss the opportunity for a do-over every time we choose the darkness of our differences over the light of our common humanity. As individuals, we miss it by preferring the darkness of self-criticism over the light of self-acceptance, the darkness of judging over the light of forgiving, and the darkness of anxiety over the light of hope. Like the Sanhedrin who turned Jesus over to be crucified, we take a pass on the opportunity for a do-over when we encounter others through the filtered lens of our own bias rather than in the clear light of God's face.

Still, God is relentless. Every time we choose darkness, God offers us a do-over. For God so loves the world that God sends God's only Son. Every time we gather for Eucharist, every time we sit and listen to the gospel, and every time we come forward to share in communion, we're saying YES to this do-over. And maybe one day we'll muster the courage to accept it. Maybe one morning we'll get up and realize we can let go of the darkness, start anew, and shape a future of light for ourselves, our families, and our world.

Green Is a Good Color for Anger

The boy looked at me with tears welling in his eyes. At first, I assumed he was expressing sadness and disappointment, but I quickly realized he was fighting back tears of frustration. He simply didn't understand. The large red S- with a frown next to it bullied him from the top of the homework paper. It was more than his six-year-old mind could take in.

I lifted him onto my knee and held him close while we talked a little about the paper and a lot about his emotions. The homework sheet was a mess. It had been a very simple assignment asking him to color a picture of the main character in a story they had read in school. The image, which started as a simple outline of a girl, looked like an explosion in a guacamole factory. He had taken a green crayon and scribbled over everything. The girl's hair, face, shirt, hands, feet—all a sloppy mess of green that looked like a drunken leprechaun. Either he thought the assignment wasn't worth his time and attention or something else was going on. Regardless, he clearly believed an unsatisfactory mark was offensive. So we talked.

A few weeks later I pulled the paper out during a parent/teacher conference and asked Mrs. Svoltman to help me understand why she felt it was necessary to grade such work. Yup, I set aside all my pontificating about letting children fail and became *that* dad.

Mrs. Svoltman looked at me as though I was missing half my brain. She recoiled visibly and her eyes narrowed. The answer was obvious to her. "Well, just look at it. He's capable of doing much better work. I mean, here..." she shuffled through a file and produced other examples of his work. "He normally does a much better job. This was an unsatisfactory effort."

I nodded. It was out of character for him. "Did you ask him about it?"

"No," she confessed before explaining, "I didn't have to. It's obvious he didn't try."

"Yes. Well, I asked him about it." I told her about the conversation we had, about how he thought the girl in the story had been treated unfairly and that she would probably feel angry. Green, he had reasoned, was a good color for anger, so he smothered her image in a volatile eruption of a color I can only describe as seaweed.

He had actually done exceedingly well on the assignment but was judged negatively because his execution did not conform to Mrs. Svoltman's expectation. He had colored an expression of the girl's inner state rather than her outer state.

How often do we do this? How often do we judge someone else based on the eyes we see through without opening ourselves to the heart they live through? I'm sure I've done it a thousand times. Before seeking to learn more about another person's story and perspective, we measure against our own thought process and deem them to be satisfactory or unsatisfactory. In response to an op-ed piece I once wrote about immigration, I received a vitriolic letter accusing me of being a heartless capitalist who defends immigrants only so I can exploit cheap, illegal labor. Wow, I thought at the time. Wow. Clearly, someone was looking at the world through jaded lenses and projecting their tint onto me.

Mrs. Svoltman glared at me with a look I hadn't received from a teacher in over twenty years. I could feel her project a big red S- onto my forehead. Finally, she said, "He could have made an effort to be neater about it."

"Anger isn't a very tidy emotion, is it?" I countered.

The Quieting of Joe Hammer

Our Scriptures don't tell us much about Joseph before he met Mary and agreed to raise Jesus. Actually, they don't tell us anything. Fortunately, archeologists found his high school yearbook among the Dead Sea Scrolls, Bethlehem Class of -09. Just kidding. They used the Hebrew calendar. It was actually the Bethlehem High Class of 3751. Go Spartans! According to the yearbook, Joseph was a fine student who spent most of his time in shop class, where he was given the nickname Joe Hammer.

He served on the stage crew for the school musical (*Joseph and the Amazing Technicolor Dreamcoat*), and he was a varsity track athlete who went to state for the long jump, but he was best known for the vehicle he drove—a '41 Mercury Dromedary with a Windsor double hump 351 V8 that would paste you against the seat when you kicked it, a fact that could be considered either good or bad depending on where you stood on the issue. But while Joe did his best to keep the speed down, he lived with the volume up. He ripped out the camel's AM radio and installed a Blaupunkt AM/FM 8-track stereo, which of course blasted too much power for the factory-installed speaker. Being the shop fly that he was, Joe wired a set of console speakers strapped onto the back. You could hear music blasting by bands such as Genesis and Exodus when he was still 350 cubits away, except for the time when the Dromedary needed a muffler.

Tucked in the clay jars with the yearbook were various excerpts from Joseph's personal blog, which archaeologists have pieced together to give us more of his story.

By the time Joseph met Mary, he had settled down. The Dromedary was history, long since replaced by a beige Dodge

Caravan with a satellite receiver and MP3 interface, which was very cutting edge since the MP3 format, like the Gregorian calendar, hadn't been invented yet. But he rarely cranked the volume anymore, preferring instead to drive in silence. The difference was not that he liked music less, but that he valued quiet more. And that's not because he'd gotten older, he insisted; it's because he'd gotten wiser.

"Musicians tell us it's the silence between the notes that makes the music," Joseph would say philosophically over wine with friends. "Artists tell us negative space gives dimension to positive space. If you want to make a point and have it resonate, you'll master the art of..." he'd take a sip from his goblet and let it hang in the air for a moment before continuing, "the pause." He was right in a timeless way. Even today, when we want to pay tribute to someone's life, we offer a moment of silence.

This is where we find God—in the stillness. But we have to quiet our minds and listen. Joseph had been inspired by the Books of Kings, where Elijah first looked for God in the cosmic expressions of might and power—heavy winds, earthquakes, and fire—but came up empty. Finally, Elijah found God in a tiny whisper. This story left a profound imprint on Joe, who won Mary's heart on their first date when he said, "We're more likely to find God in the wings of a butterfly than in our stresses and anxieties, but where do we place most of our attention?"

Later, when Joseph awoke from a dream and told Mary they had to travel the long way home, routing all the way through Bum-Gone-Egypt, because King Herod wanted to kill Jesus, Mary knew to pay attention and listen. Sure, it struck her as a little far-fetched at first, but then she recalled how centered Joe was. His still waters ran deep, so if in the quiet of the night and in the depth of his prayer, that's what he heard an angel tell him, well, that was more than enough for her. They'd go live in Egypt a while, even if they had to stay there until Herod died.

At long last, as the small family made their way back toward Nazareth with the Caravan loaded with toys and Goldfish crackers, Mary looked at her husband and said, "It's really good to be going home. But anywhere we go feels like home as long as I'm with you."

Joseph reached over and held her small hand. They drove on in silence. Eventually he spoke, "I know all this time in Egypt was very difficult and lonely, but it really means a lot to me that you trusted me."

Mary smirked in that simple, cute way with her chin down and her eyes up. It always made Joseph glad to be alive. "I admit," she said, "that I thought you were a little crazy at first. But then when I considered how well you balance the noise in the world with quiet meditation, I realized you're the least crazy man I know."

"For the record," Joseph responded, "if I still had the Dromedary, we could have outrun all of Herod's chariots. They never would have caught us."

Fusion vs. Friction

Leslie is stoic about most things. She rides life's waves, taking stormy weather and bad coffee in stride. When her niece vomited tomato soup on her white sofa, she calmly comforted and held the child before cleaning it up. "It's just a couch," she would say later. "It's not like it has a soul." She is unflappable about nearly everything. Except dogs. Leslie loves dogs. Their loyalty, unconditional love, selfless nature, gentleness, everything. In Leslie's mind, dogs generously provide examples from which humanity could learn. A lot.

Leslie is the right hemisphere of my brain.

Jackson Ethan Thomas, or "Jet" as most people call him, lives across the hall from Leslie. He's more of a cat guy. While Leslie listens to a lot of country hits and '80s rock, Jet sticks to classical and instrumental jazz. "Leave the lyrics to the poets," he shared in a hallway conversation with Leslie. "I listen to relax, not to jump around." Jet, as you would imagine, is a little high-strung and needs to keep things in order.

Jet is the left hemisphere of my brain.

Needless to say, Leslie and Jet fell in love. It was inevitable. Opposites attract, so they were either going to repulse each other or complete each other. That's how life works. And since neither had much room in their hearts for hatred or repulsion, they ended up with a Cape Cod on a cul-de-sac with three kids, two dogs, and a cat named Compromise.

It's a real kick when things that seem opposed to each other, complete incongruities, come together to make something new and better. A taco salad. Romeo and Juliet. Surf and turf. I love how the north and south poles of a magnet create the electricity that powers the world, how sun and rain drive photosynthesis, how male and female, Mars and Venus, come together to cocreate new life with earth spinning in the middle.

When two forces bump up against each other, one of two things is going to happen: friction or fusion. They're either going to collide or unify. When they feed friction, we end up with a duality of wars and wills, Hatfields and McCoys. They divide and sow seeds of repulsion and intolerance. But when they fuse, brilliant and loving energy is released into the world. The sun, which makes life on earth possible, is a super-giant fusion reactor.

Our ancient stories advise and instruct us to choose fusion over friction when we're faced with conflict. David, for example, was given two chances to defeat Saul, but chose instead to unite with him. That fusion, of course, built the foundation for the great nation of Israel. Imagine what could happen if the members of Congress followed that example. Wow. That might actually be constructive.

Let your mind rest there for a moment.

Over and over the gospels advise fusion over friction. Don't escalate the conflict; reconcile it. To make the point clear, Jesus repeats it in several ways: turn the other cheek, love your enemies, do to others as you'd have them do to you, be merciful, stop judging, and stop condemning. In other words, don't get caught up in the things that divide and separate; invest your energy in the things that unify and harmonize. Don't feed friction; foster fusion.

Jesus lived in a time in which divisions and distinctions governed the social order. He rejected them all. So he spoke to the Samaritan woman at the well: fusion. He dined with tax collectors and prostitutes: fusion. He reached out and touched lepers: fusion. Thus St. Paul writes that in Christ there is no rich or poor, slave or free, male or female, Jew or Gentile—we are all one body of Christ. Unified and fused.

It all sounds heavenly, because it is. What holds us back from living this way? Well, there's the rub. We'd have to let go of ego. We'd have to accept dog people as dog people and cat people as cat people, and stop trying to convince everyone to be, think, act, and speak like us.

Heaven Is as Simple as a Hug

A few years ago, I was presiding at a wedding that included a three-year-old ring bearer. Three-year-olds, to put it mildly, are unpredictable and easily overwhelmed. So are many grooms, but that's for another story. To help manage the situation, the bridal party had adopted a common reward scheme used at other weddings, whereby they armed the best man with a bag of gummy bears, and instructed the little boy to walk up the aisle to get the gummy bears from his Uncle Jeff. Things went smooth as glass at rehearsal. The kid got the gummy bears. Victory for everyone.

At the wedding the next day, the little boy, dressed in strange clothes in this strange place among all these strange people, walked up the aisle expecting a reward from Uncle Jeff. But no one had thought to bring a second pack of gummy bears. They only had one pack and had burned it off at rehearsal. So there we were. The wedding party was standing in the front of the church waiting for the bride. In a moment of frozen panic, the ring bearer teetered on the threshold of a complete meltdown. A singular collective breath was held. The maid of honor tugged on my vestments and whispered, "Where are the gummy bears?" My astute and pastoral response was (shrug) "I don't know." And then the tantrum hit, the wailing and grinding of teeth. The child had done what was asked. He had walked the path as told but didn't receive the promised reward.

Around that same time, I presided at another wedding, also including a three-year-old ring bearer (the bride's nephew), but no promise of gummy bears. Rehearsal went fine; the child did what was asked. But the next day at the wedding, dressed in strange clothes in a strange place among all these strange people, the panic started in the back of the church. Everyone held their breath. Would there be a meltdown? Without missing a beat, the groom, who was standing in front waiting for the arrival of his bride, simply walked down the length of the church to the back, got down on one knee, gave the child a hug, wiped his tears, gave him a second hug, and then picked him up and carried him to the front of the church. Oh my—hearts melted. Cameras flashed. Women swooned. This, my friends, is the kingdom of God.

Jesus keeps trying to explain this to people—the kingdom of God is not a reward; it's rewarding. It's not a noun; it's a verb. It's not a place; it's a disposition of heart, a way of life. It's the tiny little seed we plant in the garden that grows large and gives great life. It's the pinch of yeast we knead into the dough that makes the bread rise and feed the multitudes. It is every action and experience of love we put in motion that lasts forever.

We have a hard time getting our heads around this because we were introduced to the idea of heaven when we were small children, and we were told it is a reward, like gummy bears. But we're not small children anymore. We should be coming from a desire to love as Christ loves us, not coming because we want the candy. So Jesus tells us, "Look, if you don't change your heart here, you're going to show up and the Lord's going to look at you and say, "I don't even recognize where you're coming from. I mean—are you coming from a place of entitlement? Are you coming from a place where you think you've earned a reward? Are you coming from a place of self-interest?" And we're going to say, "How do you not recognize us? We ate and drank with you." And he will say, "That may be so, but you're not coming from the giving heart of love." And like the three-year-old who didn't get his gummy bears, there will be wailing and gnashing of teeth.

Look around at the culture we've created. Are we acting more like loving Christian adults with empathy and compassion for the least among us? Or are we acting more like children wanting to get the candy we think we deserve? Love expects nothing and gives everything. And that's rewarding.

Knowledge

I Danced with Rebecca

I danced with Rebecca. With my left hand in her right, and my right on the tender curve of her waste, we spun a stiff-legged polish hop around the small hardwood floor inside Jerome's Country Bumpkin. This was church, or the aftermath thereof, Bakerville style. When Saturday evening Mass at Corpus Christi went forth among the people, a small stream of headlights divided the cornfields lining highway B, intending to go forth among the people at the Bumpkin. My father's shiny black Marquis Brougham was among the last boats in this ritualized regatta.

On this particular summer night, Dad let me drive the downhill mile from the church to the sanctuary, as we used to say. By the time our family spilled through the screen door, the jukebox was pouring out polkas, and the beer pitchers were pouring out Pabst, though I suspected in reverse order. I spied Rebecca's straight blonde hair and round face bouncing near the dartboard and, just like that, I was darn glad to be a sixteen-year-old Catholic boy.

These were our people. Farmers, electricians, and diesel mechanics. Looking into their faces, you could see life chiseled into sun-carved crevices. No pretenses. No posturing. No need to judge or be judged. They were at my confirmation, my high school graduation, and my wedding. They made casseroles and brownies when my grandfather died, and when Kenny's wife, Marlene, was diagnosed with non-Hodgkins lymphoma, they prayed together, cried together, and found a way to laugh together when Kenny needed it most.

This is where I learned community. And while it may seem more romantic and idyllic in retrospect than it did in experience, it was real nonetheless. In fact, it was nothing but real. The transition from church to life and back again was cornsilk smooth. I feel not enough time has passed for me to say this, but here goes: parish communities like this rarely exist anymore. The idea of a small, white church on a country hill is as quaint as malt shops and ten-cent candy bars. When Fr. Charlie retired, the parish was relegated to "mission" status, a franchised outpost of a large parish in the nearby city.

For the first time in a couple of generations, Corpus Christi was served by a priest who didn't have a first name, had never put his back into a shovel, and wouldn't toss his loose change onto the polished pine bar at the Bumpkin. People lost interest and, with it, connection. Mass attendance waned. Fr. Charlie may have given dry, uninspired homilies, but he did it with a smile and, overall, he was relevant. He spoke Bakervillian like a native and knew the value of a well-placed "damnit."

People coincidentally worshiping within the same space do not necessarily form a community any more than the congregants of shoppers at Kroger's do. It's safe to say, then, that a spirit of community does not automatically result from people who happen to be doing the same thing in the same place at the same time. There is decisively more to it. Perhaps churches get the cause and effect confused at times. Jesus and his renegade group of unlikely ragamuffin followers did not form a community as a consequence of gathering in the same room to celebrate Passover. They gathered and broke bread together to reaffirm and express the community they shared with each other on the road, in the streets, and on the seashore.

So it was among the parishioners at Corpus Christi. Their lives were intertwined in many ways by virtue of shared experiences. They farmed adjacent fields, sent their children to the same schools, were often related by blood or by marriage, belonged to the same 4-H club, and spent their Friday nights at the same high school football games. Against such a backdrop, there was no point in being pretentious because everyone knew you too well. If you tried leaving your brokenness at home when you came to Mass, chances are one of your neighbors would drive into your yard, pick it up, and bring it to church on your behalf. Religion was the expression, not the cause, of community.

The nostalgic notion that church life used to be, and perhaps ought to be, the center of community is perhaps naive. One could make the same assertion about the barbershop, local saloon, or general store, all bygones except in very small towns. Yet an experience of holy community is central to an experience of Holy Communion. Such a community must be authentic, not fabricated or contrived; this is a tall order for a culture that pays top dollar for fabricated and contrived experiences—a la Disney and Vegas. So where does church fit in the contemporary world? How do we foster the meaningful and genuine sense of holy community essential to being one body of Christ?

Even in this great age of individualism, people still form and value communities. They may be fantasy baseball leagues and book clubs, but they are active communities nonetheless. A key difference in today's context when compared to that of a few generations ago, however, is that people now participate in communities by choice, not by default. The parish church model has yet to come to terms with this. Still, some things will never change. Put a boy and a girl by a dartboard and crank up the music, and both will become believers. Stated more politely, parish communities thrive when church, like the gospel itself, is about life.

Thank You, Mr. Holland

There's a great scene in the movie *Mr. Holland's Opus* in which one of Mr. Holland's band students is struggling in her attempts to play the clarinet. Technically, she's quite proficient, but the music just doesn't flow for her. No matter how diligently she practices, she grows increasingly frustrated until she's ready to quit and give up. Finally, Mr. Holland takes the sheet music away and tells her to play with her eyes closed. She objects vehemently. How can she make music without the music? "There's more to music than notes on a page," he tells her. "It's about heart, and feelings, and moving people."

Sometimes our spirituality is like that. We are tempted by the security of the page, focusing on the black-and-white markings, the rules and the rubrics. But life is really about heart, and feelings, and moving people. It's about four-year-olds with Kool-Aid moustaches, grandparents getting misty at weddings, and strangers making momentary and mysterious eye contact as they pass at the market. If you listen to Mozart's *Requiem* but only hear the technical components—the notes and measures, you'll never enter the music. You'll hear it, but you won't enter it. And if you look at faith but see only the observable facts, you'll never enter the full substance of truth. There's a huge difference between the two. The facts say I am a father of three young men; the truth is that as I watched my sons wash each other's feet on Holy Thursday, I was moved to tears. The facts point to buds on the trees behind my house; the truth reveals the miracle of God's creation constantly bursting to life all around me. The observed universe (fact) might leave us speechless at times, but it is far less inspiring than the experienced universe (truth). "Heard melodies are sweet," Keats wrote in *Ode on a Grecian Urn*, "but those unheard are oft sweeter."

This is an ancient theme in many Eastern and Western spiritual traditions. We find it in the Buddhist Dhammapada, in Iroquois Longhouse Religion, and in the Christian celebration of Holy Week and the Easter Season bridging life, death, and resurrection. On Palm Sunday, when we hear Pilate say to Jesus, "Truth! What is truth?" he is dismissing all meaning beyond the obvious and apparent. But Jesus is only interested in depth and substance. In Luke's account of the Easter morning story, we get it again. Mary Magdalene runs to tell the other disciples the truth revealed to her through direct experience—that Jesus lives—but they don't believe her. They want factual evidence. Peter takes off and runs to the tomb to observe with his own eyes. And in a post-resurrection account, it's Thomas who refuses to accept the truth. He won't believe until he has empirical, three-dimensional, factual evidence. When Jesus says, "Blessed are those who have not seen and yet believe," he's not talking about blind faith. He's talking about those who see the miracle of life, not just the buds on the trees. He's talking about those who feel the music rather than just see the notes.

Isn't this ultimately what life is about, where deep joy is found? This is what it means to be Easter people. Prayer is not about the words. Faith is not about bowing or kneeling. And spirituality is not about candles and rosaries. The value of all those external actions and objects, perhaps their only real value, is found in the degree to which they inspire the heart and move us to experience a deeper love. It's not about the fact of life in the next world; it's about the truth of love in this and all worlds. This is why Jesus lived—to show us how to love. This is why

Jesus died—to show us the depth of love. And this is why Jesus rose—to show us the infinite miracle of love. His life, death, and resurrection empower us to let go of the anxieties and stop worrying about the superficial. He frees our minds, our hearts, and our souls to live in the full experience of his love now and forever. The music is already within us.

So What Do We Hang On To?

Standing by the window and looking out at the yard, both hands cradling a cup of very black coffee, Jeffery was struck by the thick carpet of leaves strewn across the lawn. He was especially impressed by nature's ability to distribute them relatively evenly. He took a sip and nodded approvingly, although it wasn't clear if he was affirming the coffee, the yard, or both. "If this were a Hallmark movie," he called to Jenn, "a team of art directors and set designers would have spent a week trying to achieve what God seemed to accomplish overnight. And it would look fake." It was a forced observation, but he never passed up an opportunity to needle Jenn by mocking Hallmark movies. Turning his eyes upward, he noticed more leaves still clung to the trees than had fallen to the ground. How deep would they pile, he wondered, if he waited until all had fallen before raking?

This was an annual autumn argument at his house. Each October he would lament the futility of raking the leaves when so many more had yet to fall. Jenn would respond wryly that it's futile for him to have a perspective different from hers. After thirty-nine years of marriage, he had to admit she was right about that. As with every autumn, they would rake the lawn three or four times before all the trees had shed their foliage, but it was a job they shared, a seasonal rite reminding them of the life they built and maintained together. Years earlier, it had been an annual family event with children rolling in the yard and jumping in the piles. Now it was just Jeff and Jenn, still smiling and making eye contact over the noise of a leaf blower.

Counting all the leaves on all the trees—maples, oaks and birches—would be like trying to count all the hairs on a litter of caffeinated puppies. Even a rough estimate would be a fool's errand. Still, it was a question Jenn asked every year: "How many do you think there are?" Keeping with the ritual, Jeff would pause and stroke his beard as he took a visual inventory. "Oh, there's somewhere between twenty and thirty," he'd finally observe, understating the obvious. It was a conversation as predictable as the season itself, a verbal quilt to wrap themselves in as the world changed around them. Then Jeff would observe that seven months earlier the number was easy to count—zero. And in another few weeks, it would be zero again. Such is the nature of things. The trees bloom life-giving splendor, do their work, then gracefully let go. We should be more like the trees, faithful that the Creator has it figured out so we don't have to cling with anxiety.

I'm reminded of the quote by Rumi, "Be like a tree and let the dead leaves drop." The Sufi mystic's wisdom is not so different from the passage in Ecclesiastes about a time for everything (3:1–8). Autumn in the upper Midwest reminds us of verse 6 in that sequence: "A time to seek, and a time to lose; a time to keep, and a time to cast away." Indeed, autumn is the season for letting go. How will we make room for the new life, the new hope, and the new future ahead if we are still toting around the dead weight of anger, resentment, guilt, hatred, jealousy, insecurity, and so forth? Be like a tree and let the dead leaves drop, indeed. If we feel like we keep repeating the same patterns year after year without deep spiritual growth, perhaps it's because we haven't shed the old to make room for the new. Let us not put the new wine in old wineskins.

In its own way, I imagine the autumn of my life is looking a lot like Jeff and Jenn's yard. Whether it's seen as a mess in need of a lot of work or it's seen as a tapestry of God's handiwork depends mostly on the mind-set of the observer. Both perspectives are true, I suppose. Here are a few meditative questions I find myself pondering as I walk through life's woods and kick leaves from my path: What is the dead weight I carry with me from year to year? What do I gain by holding tight and not dropping these dead leaves? What will I do with the freedom I gain by letting go?

Jeff and Jenn finished the job and gave each other a double high-five, as is their way. Over the years they had let go of a lot—their children who had grown and moved away, the youthful insecure need for perfection, abuse scars from childhood, the relentless quest for financial success, both of Jenn's parents and Jeff's father. All life is about letting go until we are finally ready to let go of life itself.

"So what do we hang on to?" Jeff asked as he stirred a little Bailey's into the two cups of hot chocolate when they were back in the kitchen. "Anything?" Jenn looked up and saw the artwork of a five-year-old granddaughter hanging on the refrigerator. It was a picture of the child and her father building a snowman the previous winter and had been hanging there since before any of the leaves they had just raked had poked through as buds. "Roots," Jenn replied. "Roots and love."

Old Milwaukee by Moonlight

As Michelle and I walked home from the campus library on an unusually warm April night in 1986, I paused in the moonlight casting a glow on the street. Things were changing quickly and the air that night begged to be breathed deeply. With final exams and graduation just a few weeks away, it would be one of the last quiet, calm evenings we would be able to steal with each other for another month or so. Looking into her eyes, I asked her to be my wife. It was that simple. And she said yes. We got engaged without a candle-lit dinner, without a string quartet, without a carefully orchestrated plot broadcast on a giant stadium scoreboard, without even a ring.

It wasn't a complete surprise. We had certainly talked about a future together, but I had wanted the timing, the setting, and the story to be perfect. Perhaps I needed the illusion of perfection to mask my own imperfections. I was flat broke, staring down a mountain of student loan debt, and I had no post-graduation employment prospects. Even during the economic boom of the 1980s, there weren't a lot of opportunities for freelance philosophers and wannabe poets. Michelle was becoming a social worker, and I wanted to be a writer, although my own fear of failure prevented me from actually writing, which it turns out is a career prerequisite. You'd think I would have understood that. Either way, my self-identity was a confused mess.

I felt somewhat irresponsible in asking someone to marry me before I had a job. I didn't even have enough money to buy a pizza, much less an engagement ring. But when I had shared my concerns with Michelle a few weeks prior, she looked at me rather incredulously and challenged, "If financial security is more important to you than our relationship now, when will it stop being more important? At what point will you ever put marriage first?" Any doubts were removed at that point. I had to marry this woman. So I asked her in the middle of the intersection where Niagra Street crosses 2nd Avenue in Eau Claire, Wisconsin. To this date, it likely stands alone as the only marriage proposal ever offered at that remarkably inauspicious but secretly romantic location.

To toast our engagement, we walked to her apartment and shared a single can of Old Milwaukee beer because I couldn't afford two cans.

The Church likes to hold marriage up as an analogy of the relationship between Christ and the Church—actually, more than an analogy. The relationship between Christ and the Church is often said to be exactly the same as the relationship between spouses—an assertion I've often thought could be advanced only by men who have never received an exasperated eye-roll from a woman who can't believe she married THAT. In your search for an inspiring role model of patience and perseverance, I'd point you toward Michelle. I don't mean to brag, but because of me a lot of people pray for her.

Three decades and three sons later, I see the early years of our relationship in a very different light. The place we started and the path we charted was something far better than perfection; it was authentic. It was us. Awkward, broken, unsure, confused—I cannot think of a better string of adjectives to describe the blessed state of the human condition, and perhaps the state of organized religion in general. What a gift it is to let go of the illusion of perfection and journey forward in authenticity!

Jesus Wonka and the Chocolate Factory

Sean drew a slow and thoughtful sip from his beer and set it back on the patio table, his hand still on the bottle. His gaze drifted toward the trees at the edge of the yard. "Remember when we were kids? Remember the movie *Willy Wonka and the Chocolate Factory?*"

"Oh, yeah," said Sr. Angela. "I loved it when that bossy little girl blew up like a giant blueberry and the Oompa Loompas rolled her away to the juicer room—You're turning violet, Violet!"

"There are days when this whole spirituality business makes me feel like little Charlie walking past Willy Wonka's Chocolate Factory before he gets the golden ticket. I can see it. I can smell it. I can even reach out and touch it, but I can't experience it. We're told that the kingdom of God is at hand. It's right here. So close, yet it seems so far away. I can see it right in front of me, but I'm just this poor beleaguered kid on the wrong side of the fence."

Sr. Angela took the bottle from Sean and poured a little more into her glass. This had been their way since she first visited him to welcome him to the parish eight years ago. "Do you want a beer, Sister?" Sean had asked at the time with a mischievous grin as though he was going to corrupt a nun. Little did he know. She called his bluff, "I'll split one with you." Thus started the most cherished Sunday evening ritual in each of their lives.

"What do you think the fence is?" she asked. "What's the barrier keeping you out?"

"Hmm... I don't know. Stress maybe? Anxiety?"

"Yeah, that certainly sounds right, doesn't it?"

The sun was beginning to set, and the air exhaled upon the neighborhood like a long, soft sigh. The weekend's energy had been spent at ballparks, beaches, and barbecues. Such is the way of things. People, repackaged into their houses, were now checking emails, doing homework, and packing Monday lunches. Weekends have a way of resetting life's rhythms, an important touchpoint that's lost when sabbath is skipped. It's only in these reflective, de-stressed moments that we're able to sit back, ponder mystery, and process our own response to the world.

"What's on the other side of the fence for you?" Sister Angela asked. "What's in your version of Wonka's chocolate factory?"

This was why Sean loved these conversations so much. She pushed him. "Well, what do I long for? Peace, probably. Peace and tranquility. And a black Trans-Am with a gold firebird on the hood like Burt Reynolds drove in *Smokey and the Bandit*, but I suppose that's a latent midlife crisis thing."

Sister Angela tipped her glass and nodded approvingly. Her uncle had raced on Midwest dirt tracks, so she grew up around fast cars and was known to have a lead foot herself, a character tidbit she kept hidden. But sitting in the chair on Sean's patio was slow-down time, so she gave his thoughts space to idle. Not every firefly needs to be chased.

It was Sean who returned to the metaphor. "You know, I had never considered that movie to be an allegory for the kingdom of God before. Does it work? In the end, Wonka gives Charlie the whole kielbasa. What's that about?"

"Hmmm...the meek inherit the chocolate factory. That sounds even better than inheriting the earth. I know I'd rather inherit a chocolate river than a polluted one." Sr. Angela smiled with self-approval.

"Oh my God, Sister," Sean laughed with mock derision. "Please tell me you're not proud of yourself for that joke."

"I am actually. Yes. I'm not usually good at dry humor."

"Well, at least you got the dry part down," he teased. After eight years of conversations like these, there was a sibling-like easy banter between them. Sister Angela relished the fact that Sean was just Sean. He didn't put up a false front the way so many people do around priests and nuns. He talked to her the way her younger brother did, and he wore the same thread-worn University of Michigan t-shirt every Sunday since he found out she came from an Ohio State family.

"Back to Wonka," Sister Angela said, "why did he give the factory to Charlie?"

Sean knew the answer to this, or at least an answer. He had pondered the question before. "Charlie inherits the Chocolate Factory because Willy Wonka sees that the Chocolate Factory is already within Charlie. Everything Wonka's life's work was about—integrity, compassion, and kindness—was already embedded in Charlie's heart."

Sister Angela drained the last drop from her glass, pushed her chair back, and leaned forward. "Looks like you found your answer, Sean. My work is done here for tonight. The kingdom of God isn't on the other side of the fence. The kingdom—the peace, the tranquility, even the black Trans-Am, the whole kielbasa as you say—is already in you."

Counsel

I Pray for Talons and Wings

There is no reasonable comparison between dehydrated beef stroganoff and fresh trout from a cold alpine lake. None. Zero. I'll give a respectful nod to the folks who manufacture and package dehydrated foods. They've come a long way and, honestly, it's not intolerable. In fact, after a long day of hiking up a steep mountain, it's almost tasty. But, come on! Fresh trout taken from the cold waters of a lake above 10,000 feet and cooked over an open fire? You can't buy a meal that tasty in all of Paris. Well, maybe you can. I don't know. I'm making that up. But it is truly memory-worthy good! So, when we go backpacking, we carry only enough packaged food to make sure we're safe. If we don't catch fish, we'll be hiking out hungry. For this reason, I am infinitely thankful for my brother-in-law, Wild Man Don, who is a far more patient, persistent, and skilled fisherman than am I.

There are days, however, when the fish simply won't bite, not even for Wild Man Don. We had such a day in Wyoming's Big Horn Mountains. For two hours we sat on rocks and walked the shoreline. Casting and reeling. Casting. Waiting. Reeling. There were a couple of phantom nibbles, but no bona fide bites. We tried nightcrawlers, spinners, leaches, flies, even the no-fail pungent-smelling magic doughballs Wild Man Don carried up the side of the mountain. When Don took off his socks, he blamed the stench on the bait that had been in his pack. It was a lie, of course, but close enough to be credible. How could any trout resist that?!

Just as I began to think there were no fish in this lake, that we were destined to eat reconstituted foodstuffs from foil pouches, an impressive osprey dove from the sky, poached a sizable fish from the lake right before our eyes, and flew off, carrying our dinner in its talons. It seemed so easy for the bird. See it. Grab it. Eat it. Like plucking a drumstick from a buffet. With this confirmation of actual fish in the lake, we continued to cast and reel. By the time another two hours had passed, we had caught three fish between the two of us, which is to say Wild Man Don caught two fish and I caught one, but who counts such trivial things as that? Either way, it was enough for a light dinner.

It's not enough merely to have faith, to believe that God will make a fish jump right from the lake into your frying pan. It doesn't work that way. You have to put the hook in the water. You have to do the work. It's also not enough to simply bait the hook and toss it in the lake. You need faith that your persistent effort will produce results eventually. The Benedictines emphasize the symbiosis of prayer and work, recognizing the spiritual need to integrate both. We cannot be nourished on one without the other.

What if Saint Teresa of Calcutta only had faith? Obviously, she was a person of faith—deep faith—but what if she only had faith? What if that's where she had stopped? What if she had said, "I care about the poor, so I'll pray that God helps them, and I have deep faith that my prayers will be answered," but then she herself never scooped even one starving child from the streets? See, Mother Teresa didn't just pray, she used her life's energy as an answer to prayer.

We can look down through history and see the pattern. What if Martin Luther King Jr. only had faith and didn't back it up with action? Or Dorothy Day? Or Gandhi? Or even Peter, Paul, or Mary Magdalene? Or what if Jesus himself had stopped at faith? All of these people had a profound understanding of the relationship between faith and action. They used prayer to transform themselves, and then they used their lives to transform the world.

That brings us to our own spirituality. James tells us faith without works is dead. Faith without action is empty and meaningless. That's big. It leaves me looking in the mirror and asking myself, "How real is my faith? Am I just going through an empty exercise? Or am I really seeking to transform myself so that my life might become an instrument to transform the world?"

I've found it's very easy to ignore my personal responsibility, to misuse faith by making everything God's problem. When we do not embody prayer through action, do we diminish its sincerity? If we pray for peace, yet harbor grudges and wage war; if we pray for the sick and the dying, yet support policies that deny equal access to health care; if we pray for the poor, yet buy clothing sewn in sweatshops from retailers who do not pay living wages, do our prayers really matter to us? Do we mean them? But when we back up our prayers with action, when we stock pantry shelves, seek reconciliation for broken relationships, take steps to reduce our carbon footprint, or visit the sick, doesn't the world feel right? When we act, our prayers feel alive and fulfilling. But without action, are our prayers sincere?

So how should we express our faith without feeling overwhelmed by and excessively responsible for all of the world's needs? How should we pray? Consider bringing three facets to prayer:

First, pray that God who is love transforms you, giving you the heart, the courage, and the wisdom to transform the world.

Second, pray that God might use your life to answer the prayers of others. We don't usually think about the way strong faith makes us both the source of and the answer to prayer.

And third, pray that God leads you in that transformation. Be open and be still so that you might listen and hear where God is leading you, how God is calling you to transform the world.

Pray for the transformation of your heart; pray that your life may be used to transform the world; and pray that God guides you in this transformation.

Go to Hell, Mephistopheles

The Trans-Siberian Orchestra's great rock opera *Beethoven's Last Night* gives us a fictionalized story of Ludwig von Beethoven having just finished his tenth symphony—his greatest and most beautiful composition. Indeed, he believes it is destined to be history's most powerful musical achievement. As Beethoven sits back to drink in this moment of supreme accomplishment, the spirit named Fate drops in to tell him he is about to die. This will be his last night on earth. Fate can be a real buzzkill like that. Dang! It's like Moses never reaching the Promised Land or the father who dies before his daughter's wedding. Fate is often generous with love but cruel with timing.

But in this case, Fate is not entirely heartless. She gives Beethoven a vision of the countless people who will be moved, comforted, and even transformed by the beauty of his life's work. These include a widow who finds peace in the *Pastoral* Symphony and a crippled child who forgets his infirmity while lost in the "Ode to Joy."

Meanwhile, Mephistopheles (the devil) cannot stand the thought of so much loveliness being brought into the world. It's too risky. If people have their hearts moved and their souls inspired, well, they might just start being kind, generous, and compassionate toward one another. Heaven forbid! They might even discover that their political differences aren't worth hating each other over. The very thought gives him hives, so he schemes up a story about how he has a claim to Beethoven's soul upon death, and, as fate would have it, death is imminent. Cunningly, the devil offers Beethoven a deal: he will release the composer's soul from eternal hellfire if Beethoven allows him to erase all of his music from humanity's memory. It's a dastardly con—serve his own best interest for all eternity or let his life's work serve humanity in perpetuity. Beethoven doesn't take the bait.

The devil tries to negotiate and then gets desperate. After a little back-and-forth, Mephistopheles grows darkly manipulative. He points to a little girl outside the window and threatens to haunt and torment this girl throughout her lifetime unless Beethoven turns over his tenth symphony. She can have a life of loving warmth or a life of cold loneliness. The choice is Beethoven's and the price is his greatest symphony.

Beethoven wrestles with the voices in his head. The lyrics of the song "Who Is This Child" express the rationalizations we all go through when asked to make a self-sacrifice for the welfare of another, especially a stranger: "I learned the trick is / that we just avoid her eyes."

To any listener who has ever avoided eye contact with a homeless beggar or has turned a blind eye to the plight of a refugee, a hungry child, or the struggling single mom next door, this coping mechanism is relatable. Simply look away and avoid having to face our shared humanity. After all, we can't save everyone, can we? Are we culpable in the suffering of other people? Surely not, right?

In the rock opera, Beethoven is anguished by this dilemma.

Finally, he seems resolved to look away. After all, it's just one single little girl; it's not as though all humanity is at stake. We hear him sing, "she is but one / and there are many more / could this one life really matter?" There is a part of us that empathizes. His logic is convincing. The child is not his responsibility. He didn't bring her into the world. For every one of her, there will be a thousand more. Should he surrender his greatest work, thereby denying who he is and diminishing the value and contribution of his own life?

Just when his mind seems to have rationalized an absence of obligation to the child, his heart takes over. He can't let it go. He can put the child out of sight and out of mind, but his heart knows. The heart always knows. Most of us were raised to understand this as conscience and to form that conscience and listen to its voice. His story is our story.

Ultimately, it turns out the devil was lying all along and had no real claim on the composer's soul. What we don't know at the end of the opera is whether Mephistopheles would have gained an actual claim had Beethoven been willing to let the girl suffer. Is our fate sealed more by the transgressions of our past, as Beethoven had feared, or by how we regard the most vulnerable in the moment, as Beethoven was tested?

In the process of advancing our own self-interest in this life and the next, we can easily forget that we are villagers who share responsibility for all God's children. Jesus' disciples certainly forgot it. They got caught up in the world of self-advancement, preoccupied with their own personal greatness. Jesus, of course, calls them back. "None of you," he says as he hoists a random child from the street, "are more important to me than this child. If you want to be great, serve this child."

Christian character is not measured by what we do to advance the self, even if we are doing it for the seemingly noble purpose of procuring an eternity with God. Even heaven can be a selfish pursuit. Rather, our character is measured by how we love those who need it most, regardless of its impact on us. For those with Christ-like hearts, the least among us inspire the best within us.

Mary's In-Laws

I wonder if Mary had in-laws. Scripture doesn't mention Joseph's brothers and sisters, nor does it reveal whether his parents were still alive. However, given the tribal nature of the culture at that time, we can assume he had plenty of extended family members who brought green bean casseroles and signature jello molds to family dinners. And, as with in-laws everywhere, they likely had all sorts of opinions—opinions of which Mary would have been acutely aware.

"If it's a boy, they're naming it what? Yeshua? Well, that's a little audacious."

"I can't believe they're going up to Bethlehem now. I mean, they've had all year."

"She acts like she's the mother of God or something. I don't even know if she can cook."

"Did you see what she was wearing? I mean, really, at this time of year?"

"I heard that kid might not even be his."

Many biblical historians question the Bethlehem narrative in the nativity story because there is no record of a Roman census at that time, and, even if there had been, Joseph would have registered in Nazareth where he lived. There would have been no need to go to Bethlehem. However, had Luke's gospel simply stated that Mary and Joseph went to Bethlehem to get away from all the relatives, we'd all be like, "Oh yeah, that makes sense. I get it."

The power of Mary's and Joseph's yes is twofold: First, it affirms what they were willing to let into their lives—full trust in God's infinite life-giving love. Second, it draws a line on what they were willing to block out—the voices of expectation and judgment. They would not be swayed by cultural and tribal pressures. Such nonconformity takes a centered strength and an open heart most of us keep journeying toward. Hopefully, as we pilgrim our way through life, we are inching ever closer. If we journey well, we discover that the rickety, ragged, cobbled-together imperfection of our own lives is exactly the spot where Christ is most able to come to life.

In her brilliant book *Rebel Talent: Why It Pays to Break the Rules at Work and in Life*, Francesca Gino draws a clear distinction between rules that matter (honesty, ethics) and rules that don't (how you dress, what you order in a fancy restaurant). Her research shows that people who keep the first set of rules but break the second set are happier, more confident, and more successful at whatever they do. Mary and Joseph stand as great examples of this. They were determined to do the right thing no matter what the neighbors and relatives thought. We think of them as faithful and obedient, but how often do we think of them as courageous, confident, and happy? They focused on faith rather than propriety, on love rather than perfection. This was a radical and rebellious way to live, even by today's standards.

Pushing All the Chips into the Pot

Adam eyed me up and shoved his tongue into his cheek. I stared stone-faced at my cards, keeping my head down. He surveyed the others. It was a ruse, and we all knew it. None of us were serious or experienced poker players, but it's fun to pretend, to act like you're a pro and you know something the others don't. As the youngest of three brothers, Adam had learned the strategy game early in life. Very early. Jacob and Alex were bigger, faster, stronger, and smarter, so Adam developed a keen sense of foxlike cleverness in order to compete. After leveraging our suspense, he matched Lauren's single chip wager and raised it five—no, wait, only three, OK, four, oh what the heck, yes, five. He was gaming us.

"Too rich for me," Jenny said as she threw her cards in. We were playing for worthless plastic chips, and pride. When we play games as a family, we never play for money or anything else that would risk upstaging the fun. Still, this is a competitive crew that takes great satisfaction in outwitting one another.

I held decent but not strong cards—three jacks and some scrap. Quite often, that's a winning hand. Adam was either bluffing and trying to scare the rest of us off, or he had a strong hand and was luring us in deep. I did the calculus. Adam rarely bluffed but was apt to overplay his hand. "What the hey," I said. "It's not real money." I went all in, shoving twenty-six chips into the pot.

When all was said and done, Adam won big, I went bust, and Jenny sat smugly for having folded early. Oh well.

"I can't believe you went all in on that," Alex said afterward. "Would you have risked that much if we were playing for money?"

"Of course not," I confessed. "It's easy to have courage when there's really nothing at stake."

In the real world, we like to hedge our bets, especially when a commitment of time or money is riding on it. We'll help out for an hour at the pancake breakfast, but we won't help organize. We don't want to commit. We'll support, encourage, and maybe throw a hundred bucks at the school fundraiser, but we don't go all in.

A life committed to love, however, asks us to push all our chips into the pot. It demands that we take the risks and become vulnerable.

We don't think about it this way when we cozy-up in front of the fire called religion, but true faith is actually about going all in. It's about bringing what you got—all you got—to the table and offering it up. "Do this in memory of me" is not just about the receiving; it's about the doing, the offering up. Crucifixion and resurrection are about going all in. It's about bringing everything to the mountain and offering it up. Marriage and parenthood, the same way—go all in. If you don't, if you hold something back so you can keep living a self-focused life like most of us did as teenagers, you're going to run into problems.

The two sets of questions we're left with are these: First, what do I really believe in? What do I believe in so much that I'm willing to go all in and commit my life to it? What will I put on my back and carry up the mountain even if it kills me? This is what gives life meaning. Second, what holds me back? What causes me to hedge my bets and not bring everything I am to the table? Fear? Pride? Anxiety? This is what takes away life's meaning.

When we sit around the table and the cards are dealt, it's ultimately not about the cards at all. It's not about who wins or who loses. It's about gathering around the table together, sharing time, and being there for one another along life's unfolding journey. One life, one baptism, one God, one love. Go all in.

Living Inside-Out

"What? You can't be serious."

"Actually I am. Quite serious in fact."

Simon shook his head in disbelief. Who did this guy think he was? It was a bizarre, over-the-top, out-of-left-field request. Clearly, this had to be a joke. "Who put you up to this? Andrew? Did Andrew set this up?"

"No," Jesus shrugged. "But I'm glad you brought him up. I want him to come, too."

"Oh, him too, huh? My right-hand man? Who's gonna captain the boat if both Andrew and I follow you around the countryside like some sort of hippie groupies?"

"Apostles," Jesus corrected him. "You will be apostles, not hippie groupies."

"Tomato, tomahto," Simon clenched one side of his jaw the way people do when they're feeling incredulous. He didn't have time for this. "Whatever. Call 'em minions for all I care. Here's the deal, see...I have responsibilities. I own a fishing boat—I'm a small businessman. Do you even understand what that means—the pressures and expectations that come with that?"

Jesus was unmoved. "There will always be excuses, bro."

"Excuses?! And where do you come off playing a bro card? We just met. You hardly even know me."

"Oh, I know you, Simon. I know you love Italian food. I know you broke your sister's bicycle when you were ten by jumping it off a ramp but blamed it on Abe Malkowitz, who wasn't even there. And I know you secretly like romantic comedies even though you won't admit it to your wife."

"That last part is not true."

"Yes, it is. You especially like *Sleepless in Seattle*. You get choked up at the end every time."

Simon stood uncharacteristically speechless. It was not in his nature to overthink anything. Mostly, he relied on his gut to read the world and tell him where to fish, what to believe, and whether it would rain. But this was weird. Too weird. This man made him feel uncomfortable, yet his presence was remarkably comforting. Rationally, this whole thing was ridiculous, but something about it made all the sense in the world.

"I also know you're a rock—Petra—a strong leader, and you have a very compassionate heart."

Pragmatism was Simon's last defense. "Well, if you know so much about me, then you know I have employees. And if we're not out on the water catching fish, they don't eat. Their families don't eat. I don't eat! I get grumpy when I don't eat. I also have a wife and a home. My taxes are due, and now my mother-in-law is living with us. That woman goes through olives like Romans go through wine."

"You sound like you're under a lot of stress," Jesus redirected in a way that was both affirming and a bit challenging. No one who is under a lot of stress likes being reminded of their stress. It's a bit like telling someone who has the flu that they look sick. They know, and hearing someone else say it doesn't make them feel better. It typically makes them feel worse. But Simon was anything but typical. He was a straight shooter who much preferred to have someone tell it like it is than dance around the truth to spare his feelings.

Simon took a deep breath with a long exhale. His shoulders drooped. "Look, camel dung is flying at me from all directions all the time. I'm sorry if I've been short with you."

"No worries, Simon. But here's the thing," Jesus paused to lock eyes. "You're living from the outside-in rather than from the inside-out. You're focused on how the world is affecting you rather than on how you're affecting the world."

He let that thought hang in the air a moment while Simon absorbed what he was saying.

"I don't know what that even means," Simon said. "I'm just going about my business, doing the best I can, trying to make an honest living. And I sure hope that's enough."

Jesus wanted to reach out and hug the man. He knew Simon needed it, but he also knew it would freak him out. They had been walking from the shore toward the market this entire time and they arrived at a local wine merchant, where Jesus motioned for Simon to have a seat as he ordered a bottle of merlot, except this was ancient Israel so it wasn't a bottle and it wasn't merlot. It was an earthen jug of jandali wine made from local grapes. He produced a small loaf from his satchel and gave half to Simon. Sitting together with wine and bread—this would be a hug in a different form.

"The things you're losing sleep over, my friend, they're all outside of you. They're the roles you fill—fisherman, husband, employer, provider. And that's all good stuff, valuable stuff. But a person can lose himself in the roles we fill."

Simon took a long sip of wine and held it in his mouth while staring at the sky. Indeed, he had lost himself. Most of his days were burned off frantically racing from one thing to the next, but he couldn't imagine a different way. Life was hard and there were responsibilities he had to fulfill. That's just how it was.

"See," Jesus continued, "you've shaped your life to fit the requirements of all these roles rather than shaping it according to the gifts you have been given to share. No wonder you're exhausted and, dare I say, a little ornery at times. Your life experience is defined by what it takes from you rather than by what you are giving to it."

Reboot

I had settled in by the window and stared blankly out at the tarmac. It had been a long week and I was road weary. The aisle and center seats were open, giving me a sense of privacy for which I was most grateful. Most happiness in life is governed by the relationship between expectations and experiences, which means that a vacant middle seat on an airplane brings disproportional joy. I closed my eyes. Hopefully, I would fall asleep and not awaken until the wheels bounced off the runway back home.

My bliss, however, was interrupted by the pilot's dry voice coming over the comm, "So, uhm, here's the ahhhh situation, folks—we had a little, uhm...a little error message pop up in the cockpit here."

A *little* error message?! We're supposed to fly 560 mph at 32,000 feet—how can any error message be *little*?!

He continued, "We're not really sure what it means, so, uhmmmm...we're going to go ahead and give it a hard shutdown and then reboot just like you would with your laptop or smart phone."

"That's it?" I thought. "You're going to just reboot the airplane like it's a video game?!"

Wouldn't it be great to be able to simply reboot life like that once in a while? Whenever we see an error message pop up in our lives, we could engage a hard shutdown and reboot. I think I'd like that. I'm certain Michelle would like to reboot me sometimes. In fact, I'm pretty sure she has tried.

Each morning when our eyes open and we welcome the new sun, we're given an opportunity for a spiritual and chronological reboot. Of course, it's difficult to think of these as hard restarts because we haven't actually gone through the hard shutdown part. We don't think of sleep that way. We carry yesterday's anxieties, stresses, prejudices, and other baggage forward. Rather than reboot and live as the best version—the Christlike version—of ourselves, we settle for a primitive and buggy version. It's as though God keeps offering us an updated operating system to run our lives—Me 56.0, but we insist on letting the far less secure, relatively unstable version of Me 14.2 run in the background.

In reference to my own life, I am guilty of slapping new paint over rotted boards and then standing back and nodding with self-approval, "There, much better." It gets me through the day but does very little to get me to a better place. Sure, I might have dropped a few pounds, but am I living and loving as the healthiest, happiest version of me?

As I sat there waiting to find out if I was on my way home or not, I played the lottery fantasy game, imagining what I would do if I won the lottery. Another popular version of the same game is Mortality Awareness, in which we imagine what we would do if we had only one month to live. This is not a psychologically helpful game to play if you are stranded on an airplane that is working through an unknown error message.

If you listen to the answers most of us give, you'll notice a subtle difference between these two games. In response to winning the lottery, we fantasize about changing things outside of ourselves, such as our jobs or our homes. Many of us imagine using the windfall to put something good in the world and to fund charity work. Mostly though, we think about changing something that's not us. In response to the mortality question, however, we are decisively more self-reflective. We talk about worrying less and loving more. We actually think in terms of a total reboot for the final stretch and living our final days the way we wished we would have lived our entire lives.

What would happen if we used each morning as a reboot? What baggage, dead weight, and negativity would we set down and walk away from? How would we love more fully and generously than we do now? How free would we feel?

Courage/
Fortitude

Star Chasers

Do you ever wonder what the neighbors must have said?

"They're doing what? Following a star? Do you know what a trip like that's going to cost? It must be nice!"

"Don't you think they're getting too old for this sort of thing?"

"Who's going to mind the store while they're off gallivanting around the globe? It's just not responsible."

"You know, if you're going to have a midlife crisis, just buy a convertible and get it over with. You don't have to chase a star across the desert for two years."

The story is scant on details, has a very weak plot, and the characters are never really developed. Imagine pitching the screenplay to a movie producer: "Well, there are three guys, probably rich guys with haughty names like Melchior, Caspar, and Balthazar, and they follow a star across the desert to find Jesus."

"Rich guys lost in the desert. Sort of a *Three Amigos* meets *Gilligan's Island* thing. It's got comedic potential. What happens?"

"I don't know. They follow the star."

"That's it?"

"Well, they meet King Herod who asks them to report back after they find Jesus so he can kill the child."

"OK, that's a compelling twist. It's not funny, but compelling. What happens next?"

"They arrive and give their gifts to Jesus."

"What about King Herod?"

"Oh, nothing really. The three guys take a different route home and never report back."

"How does it end?"

"That is the end."

"Thanks for coming in, but your story isn't memorable. We're going to pass."

But it is memorable! It's been told and retold for nearly two thousand years. Why?

Our common sense and conventional wisdom tell us to be responsible and pragmatic. Yet all of the really good stories in human history and mythology involve people chasing stars. *The Illiad* and *The Odyssey*. Moses and the Hebrews in the desert for forty years. Jesus in the desert for forty days. St. Paul around the Mediterranean. Thomas Jefferson, Thomas Edison, Cesar Chavez, Susan B. Anthony—all of them were star chasers.

So what about us? Are we star chasers? How far are we willing to journey beyond our own comfort zones into the dark forest of eye-rolls and social criticism in order to encounter the Living God? The question before us is not whether the wisdom star still shines, but whether we're willing to follow it.

Regardless of what we read in the news, the star shines as bright as ever over the value and dignity of all God's people. It shines upon a solution to homelessness, hunger, genocide, unwanted children, racism, and terrorism. It shines upon a cure to addictions, abuse, hatred, and bigotry. The star shines a message of love, hope, and forgiveness for all to see, and I'm willing to bet that when we close our eyes and look into our own hearts, we sense it. We see it. We feel it. But do we follow it?

The invitation for each of us is to identify the star that calls us by name and then chase it. To be wise men and women, we might need to let go of pragmatism at times, disregard what the neighbors think, embrace the difficulties and impracticalities of the journey, and follow the star.

American Pie

Sometimes you open Scripture and it's like, "Wow! That's a jolt with a powerful kick!" You have to buckle your seatbelt and strap on a helmet. The story of the prodigal son is like that. Its deep, multilayered meaning blows my hair back. But if you're like me—and may God help you if you are—there are other times when you open Scripture and think, "Oh, puh-lease. How did that get in? When the early church fathers sat around arguing over what to include and what to keep out of the Bible, what exactly was in their chalice?" Now, before you get all outraged over my shocking tongue-in-cheek humor at the expense of the Council of Nicea and send infuriated emails about *The Da Vinci Code* to my publisher, just take a deep breath. It's all done with a smile and a wink. Keep reading and see where this is going.

I love the rich tapestry of both the Old and New Testaments. I'm continuously amazed by the way these stories have inspired people for thousands of years. But sometimes the apocalyptic stuff, books such as Revelation and Daniel, well, it can seem a little out of left field. Come on...the cosmic battle of good and evil, the sun will be darkened, the moon will not give its light, stars will be falling from the sky, dogs and cats living together...

To really understand apocalyptic literature, it helps to step back and look at when and why it was written. The apocalyptic genre was popular for about four hundred years—two hundred years before and two hundred years after Christ. Some of it was considered inspired and thus was included in our Scriptures; much of it wasn't. Most was written to offer hope to oppressed and distressed people, and two millennia later it still has value that way. In the depths of the worst times in our lives—and we all go through tough stuff—we can cling with faith to the knowledge that God is with us. When the ground beneath us crumbles, when all hell breaks loose in our lives, when the sky really does seem to be falling, still the God who is love is there with us. Light will triumph over darkness. Good will win out over evil. Love conquers all. This hope, this belief, can get us through.

After the year 200 or so, we really don't see a good example of apocalyptic writing until 1971 when Don McClean wrote "American Pie." We know "American Pie" is apocalyptic because it's filled with all sorts of bizarre things that are hard to understand. I know what you're thinking...if being filled with bizarre things that are hard to understand makes something apocalyptic, then don't marriage and parenthood also qualify? And, frankly, isn't life itself apocalyptic? To this, I say *yes*! It certainly is. Each of our lives is its own Book of Revelation.

Interpreted this way, think about how the lyrics of "American Pie" apply to your own life, how they reveal the tension between the music that wants to make you dance (love and faith) and the realities of a world filled with *bad news on the doorstep* (destruction and pain). We want to love all people as Jesus did; we want to live with mercy and forgiveness; we want to live lives of selfless servitude. But with all the hurt, hatred, and pain swirling around us, it often feels safer to spiritually cocoon within the self, to care only about myself and my own.

In the song, the desire for music—the desire to love—is ultimately overwhelmed by darkness, and it dies. The rest of the journey is spent trying to reclaim love and faith only to discover it's too late. The music (love) gasps its last breath. We're left wondering whether our failure to place our faith in love is what killed it. At the end of the song, even the Holy Trinity has no reason to stick around when we turn our backs on love.

> *The three men I admire most,*
>   *the Father, Son and Holy Ghost,*
> *They took the last train to the coast,*
>   *the day the music died.*

The apocalypse expressed by Don McClean in "American Pie," just like the apocalypse expressed by the prophet Daniel, reminds us that we have a choice. Every day of our lives we participate in the cosmic battle of good and evil by choosing between light and dark, between life and violence, between love and fear. Will we feed the hungry or will we feed our egos? Will we tear down walls or will we build fences?

The stories of apocalypse might sound daunting, but they give us hope by reminding us we have a choice. They also give us challenge by letting us know that the battle ground in the fight between good and evil is the human heart. Our hearts. Apocalypse isn't Armageddon. It's not a single event that will happen at the end of time. It's an everyday reality in our lives.

Love will conquer all when we believe in it enough to choose it.

Life as Philip on the Fourth Tee

Philip, Thomas, Bartholomew, and Simon the Zealot were taking advantage of a rare day off to play a round of golf. Phil, Tom, and Bart had wanted to play on the previous Saturday, but Simon, being zealous and all, thought golfing on the Sabbath would be a rules violation. Even though there is no specific reference to golf in the Torah, he drew their attention to the rabbinic prohibition against walking more than 2,000 cubits outside the city. No one was sure how many cubits would be walked during a round of golf or whether the 2,000 cubits was a straight linear figure or an aggregate total, but the prohibition against carrying anything on the Sabbath would require they bring caddies. Tom pointed out that the way Simon swings his clubs could be interpreted as threshing, which was also forbidden on the Sabbath, so that could be a problem. Finally, Bart suggested they ask Jesus, but all were afraid he would launch into a lengthy and confusing parable instead of giving a straight answer, so they elected to wait for another day. Today was that day.

As Phil lined up his tee shot on the fourth hole, Bart made his obligatory "watch out for the bunker" comment. It was funny the first time, since they lived on the edge of the desert and their entire world was a giant sand trap. No one even chuckled anymore. The fairway bent sharply around a stand of olive trees, so Phil paused to ponder whether he should try to punch his shot over the trees and land on the fairway on the far side, or if he should play it safe and lay-up, hopefully in the center of the bend. Seeking advice, he turned to the others, "Do you guys think I can clear those trees?"

"I doubt it," Tom teased.

"A real mensch would," offered Bart in an attempt to egg him on.

"Seriously?" Phil asked. "My integrity and honor are defined by whether I take the riskier shot or the safe shot?"

Bart was exaggerating, of course, just to needle Phil a bit. "Yes. In this moment, yes."

"Don't listen to him," Tom chimed in. "It's only the fourth hole and he's already two strokes behind. He needs you to take a couple of bad risks so he can catch up."

There was a long period of silence as all four did the mental calculus factoring distance, arc, wind, and the likelihood of Phil actually striking the ball perfectly.

"Just swing straight away like you normally do, and you'll probably slice it wildly over the trees," ribbed Simon.

Phil decided to play it safe and stay away from the trees. As they all watched the ball bounce into the rough on the far side of the fairway, Bart commented, "You golf like my grandmother who, by the way, never golfed."

Phil sighed and rolled his eyes. He enjoyed the brother-ly banter among these guys, and he knew Bart was just being Bart, but he was tired of being persecuted. It seemed everyone always had opinions on what they thought he should do, how they thought he should run his life. Sometimes it felt defeating. He wouldn't even talk to his own sister anymore because he was tired of listening to her criticisms: *When are you going to grow up and get a real job? Trim that beard—you look like a hippie. You need to stop following this Jesus guy around like some sort of a groupie.* Why couldn't they just let him be?

All around us are voices telling us we need to be a certain way in order to garner respect and approval. And very often, if we don't adhere to those standards, we're persecuted either implic-itly or explicitly. Family members are often the worst offenders. We feel compelled to conform to tribal norms lest we be judged and marginalized. Some extended family systems go so far as to ridicule anyone who chooses a healthy diet, gives up alcohol, advocates for the poor, or even goes to church. In reality, those voices are pressuring us to live in a way that validates the critic's own life choices. They attempt to rob us of the right and responsibility to live the life we each feel called to live.

The gospel reminds us that such is the price of being true. If we're going to honor the person God calls us to be—the person God created us to be—we'll need to put up with some persecution. Sometimes it will come from the media or pop culture. Sometimes it will come from peers and coworkers. And sometimes it may even come from our own families.

Faith begins with the strength and wisdom to resist the voices of criticism that tell us we're not tall enough, not smart enough, not rich enough, not refined enough, not thin enough, not holy enough...it's always something. Such voices are not from God. At times, a voice of correction might be, but not criticism. God does not criticize God's own creation. Our own creation stories tell us God looks upon those God has created and says, "This is very good."

If we're going to be authentic Christians, we have to resist false images of ourselves, make ourselves vulnerable to a little persecution, and accept that I am who I am. The next step is to openly accept others just as they are without criticism.

In Frodo We Trust

There are two voices dwelling inside of me: Esteban Diego, driven by passion and purpose, and Stefan Jakob, driven by reason and responsibility. Esteban is more likely to pack another scoop of ice cream onto the cone while Stefan is busy calculating the calories in the first scoop. Esteban lives by the mantra "Life is a joyride," while Stefan very calmly says, "Play it safe and keep your speed down." They often fight for the wheel.

On the morning of my ordination, Esteban Diego and Stefan Jakob got into a fist fight at the foot of the sanctuary. My name had been called, and I was to ascend the stairs and take my place. There I stood in the cathedral aisle, frozen in time while Esteban and Stefan had one final knock-down, drag-out fight.

With the reason, calm, and control of a skilled hostage negotiator, Stefan firmly commanded, "Now, don't panic. Be reasonable about this. Simply turn around, walk straight out the back door, and put this nonsense behind you."

"We've been through this!" exclaimed Esteban. "Have courage and faith, man! Listen to the voice of the spirit and go forward!"

"If you do, there's no turning back." Stefan was persistent and made good points. "Seize back the power and control over your own life."

My family, friends, and a cathedral full of people supportively waited in pews while Esteban and Stefan got into an epic existential argument about freedom. What does it mean to live freely: To throw yourself with abandon into the fires of vocation and purpose? Or to run into the open air where you can breathe without the weight of obligation?

I flashed back five years to the start of my formation journey. It was a day like none other, September 11, 2001, when I walked into an office in the Green Bay diocese and signed my name to officially register for a class that would launch the pilgrimage toward the foot of these sanctuary stairs. Earlier that morning thousands of people ran from the World Trade Center into the open air, while hundreds of firefighters ran up the stairs into the towers. Both were pursuing freedom of different forms. One group was running toward the freedom of the open air; the other was running toward the freedom of mission. Both groups had hearts pounding with fear and anxiety; both had to focus their life's energy on what the moment called them to. During the course of a lifetime, the moment calls us to different things at different times. As my own heart pounded with fear and anxiety, the question I faced was simple: what was the moment calling me to?

Near the end of the movie *The Lord of the Rings: The Two Towers*, Frodo is just about ready to give up on his journey. He is tired and weary from fighting the forces of darkness and his foil, Smeagol. He has to make a choice about whether to continue forward or turn back. For Smeagol, freedom is found in possessing the precious ring and all the power and control it offers. For Frodo, freedom can only be found in the risk of driving toward the fires that will destroy the ring of power. But is it worth it? Will Frodo find the strength to lift himself forward and fulfill his purpose? Will he run toward the fire or from it?

His companion, Sam, speaks with the wise but innocent voice of love as he encourages Frodo with these words:

> It's like in the great stories, Mr. Frodo. The ones that really matter. Full of darkness and danger, they were. Sometimes you didn't want to know the end. How could the end be happy? How could the world go back to the way it was when so much bad happened? But in the end, it's only a passing thing. The shadow, even darkness must pass. A new day will come. And when the sun shines, it will shine all the clearer. Those were the stories that stayed with you and meant

something, even if you were too small to understand why. But I think, Mr. Frodo, I do understand. I know now. Folk in those stories had lots of chances of turning back, only they didn't. They kept going because they were holding onto something...that there's some good in the world, Mr. Frodo, and it's worth fighting for.

Esteban Diego is the voice of Frodo in my life, tipping the balance toward the inner life, encouraging me to step into the moment and follow the call seeded within my heart. Stefan Jakob is Smeagol, tipping the balance toward the outer life, telling me to act in my own self-preservation, which has a rather devious way of sounding so rational.

Esteban won the day and I went forward, not because it was the reasonable thing for me to do, but because it was the right step for me to take when standing on that threshold. There is always something holding us back, something working to convince us that peace, comfort, tranquility, and the end of all suffering lies in the world outside of our own souls. Such is not true. If we listen to that voice, happiness will forever elude us, and we will end up torn apart and destroyed like Smeagol.

Listen instead to the spirit voice whispering from within and all will be well. Be like Frodo, who followed his heart without delay.

Mom Knows Best

In the story of the wedding at Cana, there's this nifty little exchange we often glance over. After Mary informs Jesus that the wine has run out, Jesus responds, "Woman, how does your concern affect me? My hour has not yet come." To the twenty-first-century reader, this seems rather dismissive and even disrespectful. Did Jesus really talk that way to his own mother?

Here's the beautifully poetic part—Mary ignores him. She simply turns to the servers and says, "Do whatever he tells you." She is unphased by his response. I love that about her.

There are two possibilities here. Either Jesus is serious but his mother won't let him get away with it, or Jesus is just giving his mother a hard time and she knows it. Either way, Mary is one step ahead of him. What a delightful insight we are given into the relationship between mother and son.

If Jesus is serious, his words are intended to let his mother know that he's a man now, not merely her little boy, and he will decide for himself when he's ready to reveal his identity. I watched this same scenario play out each time one of my sons came home from college for the first time. They each went out of their way to let their mother and me know they were independent and in charge of their own lives. Maybe they'll be home for dinner; maybe they won't. Maybe they'll spend the evening with us, but maybe they will make other plans. They would intentionally not communicate in a passive-aggressive way. I'm sure I did the same thing myself at that life stage. It's rather comical to observe because no matter what the young man says, Mom's still in charge and he knows it. If Jesus was trying to send his mother a message, her response sent a much more poignant one. You can be your own man, but Mom still knows best.

The other possibility is that Jesus was just giving his mother a hard time to see if he could get a rise out of her. As a young man, this little game provided constant entertainment for me. I would throw out statements that challenged every value Mom had taught me just to see how she would respond: *I don't believe in God. Marriage is ridiculous and archaic. Faith is for people who don't want to think.* I didn't actually mean any of it, or at least not all of it. It was a game to see if I could rile her, or maybe to see if her convictions ran deep enough to argue. My mother, like Mary, saw right through her son and typically ignored me. She wouldn't take the bait. I was blessed to have such a patient and intelligent mother.

In this little exchange nested in the Cana wedding story, we get a glimpse into the sacred relationship between the mother and the son. We see what a steady, strong, and resilient woman Mary was, and how marvelously human her relationship with Jesus was. Sometimes we put both Mary and Jesus on such high pedestals that we no longer identify with them, which ironically defeats the whole point of incarnation. Jesus, born of Mary, came to be one with us and among us, not one above us or apart from us.

The net effect of all this is a literary pearl tucked inside the oyster. Just before the author of John's gospel reveals Jesus' first miracle, he gives us this wonderful flash of Jesus' very human character. Yes, he's divine, but he's also remarkably human.

Arthur on the Inside

The townspeople all snickered when Arthur didn't even bother to put a foot against the rock. Either he was utterly naive or ridiculously stupid. There was no way he'd be able to pull that sword from the stone without the leverage of at least one of his legs.

Ever since it had been declared that any man able to draw the sword from the stone would become king, gallant, strong young men from near and far had given it a go. With double-fisted grips, bulging arms, and strong backs, they had tugged, twisted, wrenched, and pulled with all their might, but the thing wouldn't budge. Now Arthur shows up, puts one hand on the hilt, and doesn't bother to even put a foot against the rock? You couldn't take him seriously.

Imagine the gasps when he drew the blade from that stone with a single, smooth motion. Why, news spread like Twitter on caffeine.

Arthur had studied under Merlin, so he understood the problem differently. All those other guys were trying to become king by using their outer strength—they put their faith in their physical power. Arthur applied his inner strength, putting his faith in his spiritual power. Arthur was, we would say, inspired—in the spirit.

This is a very old legend, but with a timeless message: only those who put their faith in the spirit have the strength to change the world. John the Baptist recognizes this in Jesus—"I saw the Spirit come down like a dove from heaven and remain upon him." He's the guy who will change everything.

If you have faith the size of even a mustard seed, Jesus said, you can move mountains. Such is the power of the one who puts his faith in the inner strength of the Spirit.

Here's the kicker for us: as we've learned to harness the power of the external world, we increasingly put our faith out there rather than in the Spirit. More and more, we put our faith in the physical strength of internal combustion engines and bulldozers and guns and walls and annuities and hedge funds. More and more, we are like all the powerful and naive young men who tried to remove the sword from the stone with brute force. We want to muscle our way into controlling our world.

But every once in a while, someone who is inspired turns up and shows us how it's done. Two recently canonized saints, Teresa of Calcutta and Oscar Romero, each showed us the earth-shaking power of one person who is infused by the Spirit. Relying only on the inner strength of the Spirit, people who are inspired serve peace, justice, and human dignity. And boy, doesn't our world need one or two or ten or a hundred of those people right now?

Piety/
Reverence

Like a Child Reaching for Her Mother

I wore a black bow tie. For the most part, that's the most positive thing I remember from my First Communion. That, and the fact that my godparents gave me five dollars, which seemed far more exciting than the rosary my parents gave me. I also remember sitting small on the wooden pew with my elbows tucked close and my hands folded, taking every precaution to make sure my eight-year-old frame did not brush against the lacy dresses on either side. Cooties, you know. When I was confirmed nine years later, I would have preferred sitting between two girls, but Fr. Mike made us sit with our parents. A lot of very smart people will disagree with me on this, but I maintain the church got the seating chart wrong both times.

What I remember most about my First Communion was feeling overwhelmed with fear. I was afraid of doing it wrong and making Sister Mary Lucy angry. What if the Blessed Sacrament touched my teeth? What if I accidentally opened my mouth while chewing? Would I go to hell? I wasn't entirely sure where God stood on the issue, but I knew exactly where Sister Mary Lucy stood.

All this anxiety caused another problem. I had to pee. It started during the psalm and grew worse during the epistle. By the time Father Lekitas slogged into his homily, I was in full squirm mode. With both hands shoved into my pants pockets, I hoped to discreetly quell the stream at its source. Was this a venial sin or a mortal sin? Could I still go to Communion? Suddenly, a cold hand grabbed the back of my neck and I felt the pungent fire of Sr. Mary Lucy's breath in my ear. "Don't you dare touch yourself. Don't you dare. If you have to go to the bathroom, hurry up and go, but make sure to wash your filthy hands." Still grasping my neck, she half pulled and half pushed me from the pew, whispering loud enough for others to hear, "You're not going to embarrass me by peeing your pants."

During my exit melee, the back of my thumb brushed across the satin of Diane McCrystal's dress. She softly uttered, "Yuck."

In retrospect, the irony is sad. Fear and anxiety are not eucharistic dispositions. Eucharist begs to be imprinted with pure love. That's it. Pure love. Not regulations and restrictions. Not threat of eternal damnation. Why is that so hard? Admittedly, I wasn't in the upper room that night, but even with his impending crucifixion, what Jesus gave humanity in the bread he broke and the wine he poured was pure love. This is not a minor detail. It's the whole point.

Anxiety and fear had driven me to understand Eucharist in terms of *form* rather than *meaning*. Do it right or it's a sacrilege. You're not worthy of this, but you'd better qualify for it! Arguably, a pious posture emphasizes and ensures reverence. But authentic reverence can only come by nurturing love and understanding; otherwise it is not reverence at all; it is merely the same type of manipulated respect one has for an armed robber.

During a time when my own diocese was on a crusade to reinspire reverence by way of mandated postures, I was ministering the cup at Mass when an elderly lady approached. She completely ignored all of the instructions about pausing, bowing, or anything else. Instead, she shuffled forward with both hands outstretched like a child reaching for her mother. This, I thought, is the most reverential way to participate in Holy Communion. This is what pure love looks like.

The Body of Christ Is a Ham Sandwich

Lonzo postured himself as street tough. Or at least as street seasoned. I met Lonzo at about 11:30 on a Friday night in the old Ft. Howard Neighborhood on Green Bay's east side. We were out with StreetLights Outreach, making small talk with people hanging in the neighborhood. Lonzo, a wiry guy in his mid-twenties, was riding around aimlessly on a bicycle. He'd stop by our corner for just a minute or two and then dart off again. Five minutes later, he'd be back. When I saw him coming for about the fifth or sixth time, I walked forward and intercepted him before he reached the corner.

If I had learned anything on the streets, it's that people are tabernacles; they are typically locked and won't open themselves. You have to approach them reverently. Lonzo, it turned out, was in his second night of being homeless and hadn't eaten in two days. He didn't know where the shelters were or how any of the community meal programs worked, or even that there were meal programs.

He carried himself with a hardened exterior and made it clear he didn't need help. I assured him I could tell; I could tell he was self-reliant and would be OK. But I also told him that others had cut me breaks along the way, and I had a need to pay it forward. So I walked into a convenience store across the street and got him a ham sandwich and a bottle of Gatorade. When I returned and handed it to Lonzo, the tabernacle doors opened wide. Through tear-filled eyes he poured out his heart and shared his story with me. All I gave him was a bite to eat. He gave me a profound understanding of a eucharistic experience.

Perhaps we struggle to understand the mystery of Eucharist

because we focus so much attention on when it starts, on the mechanics of ritual and consecration. In the meantime, the more powerful question never gets asked: When does Eucharist stop? When does consecrated bread and wine stop being Holy Communion? As soon as you swallow it? When the Mass ends? When you get home? When does Eucharist stop being the very real presence of Christ?

Never. The answer is never. It doesn't stop. Once we've accepted this mystery into ourselves, how we see everyone and everything changes. Catholics bow before the Eucharist, genuflect before the tabernacle, and kneel in adoration before the luna-loaded monstrance, but if we don't show the same reverence for one another, why, we're reducing Eucharist to an object. When we participate in Holy Communion, we become the body and blood of Christ. And so does everyone else. That's a powerfully sacred thing.

Saint Benedict wrote that we should treat all objects in life with the same reverence we have for the eucharistic vessels, and we should always greet one another as we would greet Christ himself. Eucharist never stops unless we ourselves put a stop to it.

So while Eucharist is exceptional, it isn't an exception. It is an experience. The sacred reverence we experience as we celebrate Mass is exactly the same sacred reverence we are called to show for ourselves and everyone else every day of our lives.

Heaven Lost

My office in downtown Green Bay is on the penthouse level or, as everyone else in America calls it, the third floor. We live large here on the inland coast. I am also blessed with a huge window offering a spectacular view of the parking lot. On clear days I can see all the way to the beer trucks that park on Doty Street. If you're wondering where I get my inspiration, well, there you go.

So I was standing there, looking out, and noticed a black Jeep Cherokee with a parking ticket on the windshield. "Good," I smugly thought. It felt satisfying. My company pays good money to lease those parking spaces for employees and guests. The lot is clearly posted as reserved, with parking permits required. So I was glad to see the city's parking authority had been making the rounds and ensuring the rules are enforced. This is how order is maintained, how a community is able to function.

Then I watched as a man in a flannel shirt and dirty baseball cap stepped out of the passenger's side of that Jeep and grab the ticket off the windshield. He looked defeated—not angry or indignant—just defeated, with head hanging and shoulders drooped. A woman sat in the driver's seat with her head in her hands leaning over the steering wheel. I wondered about their story; what was going on? What brought them to this particular place and time? As I looked closer, I noticed how beat-up and rusted-out this Jeep was. One of the rear windows was stuck in the open position—in early December with cold winds blowing from the north. Immediately, I looked to see if there were any children in the back seat, but I couldn't tell.

As I thought about these people, it occurred to me that a $35 parking ticket would be a heavy burden. Thirty-five dollars could represent a big chunk of their grocery budget for the week. Or their heating bill. Or a tank of gas needed to get to work. I remembered living like that myself when Michelle and I were first married. We had nothing and drove old cars we could barely keep running. For a long time, we filled our gas tank only halfway because a hole had rusted through further up. We kept track of every mile, making certain there was enough gas to last until the next paycheck because there was no budget for more. Oh, and the gas gauge was broken, so going anywhere was a dice roll as we neared the end of the month. An unexpected expense as simple as a parking ticket was a major source of stress and anxiety. That sort of thing wore at our relationship and caused fights.

Suddenly, more than anything else, I wanted to pay the ticket for that Jeep couple. I wanted to take the stress away, so I ran from my office and raced down the stairs, but by the time I reached the lot, they were gone.

By wasting my time standing at the window in self-satisfied judgment, actually feeling righteous about their parking ticket, I missed my chance to share love with people who I think really needed it. I stood in the cold December wind feeling small. How much of my life have I wasted standing in self-satisfied judgment? How many opportunities to love have I missed because I was preoccupied with my own righteousness?

When Jesus talks about this age and the next age, or the realm of God and the realm of man, I think this is really what he's talking about. This age, this realm, this mind-set is so preoccupied with rules, structure, and order. And it's not that those things don't matter. We need parking laws or we'd risk living in chaos. But Jesus calls us to see beyond all that, to see with hearts of love. He tells us that those who attain the next level of spiritual awareness, the next realm, the next mind-set, have hearts that are not held back by the pettiness of the first realm.

The Edge of the Powder Keg

Peter wiped the perspiration from his brow and wondered what Jesus would say. It looked like a no-win situation. The crowds had gathered. Oh boy, they had crawled out of the woodwork for this one. Beneath the social murmur ran an undercurrent of ripe tension. This was a powder keg, and everyone was holding their breath to see if Jesus would light the spark.

When reading the Sermon on the Mount in Matthew's gospel, we're inclined to think all these people came with open minds and open hearts, that they had gathered eagerly to soak up whatever wisdom and insight Jesus would share. No doubt, some of them had. But most people, then as now, tend to bring preconceived notions and opinions to public conversations. They're not seeking enlightenment; they're seeking affirmation. Many of the people gathered on that sloping hillside would have come with agendas, and they wanted, nay expected, Jesus to say the things they wanted to hear.

The Romans were watching and listening. Would he incite rebellion? They hoped not. He'd better not. Although perhaps some Romans secretly hoped he would give them an excuse to bring this experiment in religious tolerance to a quick and violent end once and for all, forcing everyone to worship the Roman gods.

The Zealots were looking for a messiah who would restore

Jewish self-rule. They wanted Jesus to lead the charge to overthrow the Roman oppressors and restore the nation of Israel. Would he speak the stirring words that would inspire people to rise up?

This prospect made the priestly class chew their fingernails very nervously. In exchange for making sure the Jews capitulated to Roman rule, they were rewarded quite generously. It was a delicate social balance from which they benefited. If Jesus spoke words that spurred an uprising, the Romans would drop the hammer, destroy the Temple, seize their wealth, and rip away their privilege.

Then there were the Essenes, who wanted Jesus to advocate for a simple desert life void of, well, just about everything except prayer.

And, of course, there were the ever-vigilant Pharisees, who took careful notes and wanted Jesus to encourage a strict adherence to the law.

It seemed everyone in the crowd had an agenda, and they were looking for a leader who would fuel and validate their version of how the world ought to be.

Peter knew this wasn't simply a church picnic with people having different opinions about last week's homily while still agreeing that Mavis Williams' brownies would bring redemption to everyone. This was tense. Intense. The political climate was toxic. There was no way Jesus could appease everyone, so the question wasn't *if* he would upset someone; it was *who* he would upset. Knowing Jesus, Peter thought, he's not going to endorse any of their agendas. There is a good chance he'll upset everyone.

Jesus sat down and started. "Blessed are the poor in spirit... Blessed are they who mourn...Blessed are the meek, those who hunger and thirst for righteousness, the merciful, the clean of heart, the peacemakers, those who are persecuted for the sake of righteousness...Blessed are you when they insult you and persecute you and utter every kind of evil against you because of me."

People were dumbfounded. Had he just turned the world upside-down and inside-out? The blessing is not in shaping the world to align with the way you want it; it's in shaping your heart to align with God. It was brilliant in the way it gave hope to everyone.

Our world today isn't so different from the one Jesus lived in. We are still knotted up in tension so tight it feels like the world is about to burn. It might be a good time to take a deep breath, crack open a Bible (Matthew 5), and revisit the Beatitudes. The blessing isn't in having all the answers, getting everything we want, or having the power to shape the world to our liking. The blessing is in the searching and the seeking, in the meek and the merciful, in those with good hearts who choose peace.

Just Another Lost Boy

As the clock turned to 5 p.m. on Saturday afternoons, I'd step from behind the counter, grab a display radio from the store shelf, and tune in to two hours of theology and philosophy cleverly disguised as humor. Garrison Keillor's voice spilled from the speaker like a deep varnish drawing forth the rich grain from my wooden life. I was eighteen, a high school senior, scared to death that my future would forever be as ordinary as I was.

I was a small boy raised in a city that was too big for an average kid to stand out and too small for a shy kid to hide. Everyone knew you, sort of. They knew of you, perhaps they knew about you, but they didn't actually know you.

Standing in front of our religion class junior year, Fr. Berger assured us we were all gifted; God had bestowed each of us with dignity and talent, talent we were obliged to share. But he didn't really know me. He only knew of me and about me. I looked around and felt cheated. I had classmates who were obviously gifted in math, science, music, and athletics. But I seemed remarkably ordinary at everything. When we ordered class rings that spring, we were told to select an icon representing one of our talents to have embossed on the ring's side. This requirement left me feeling empty. I had no idea what to select. Nothing seemed honest. I had no discernible talent.

But Keillor's *Prairie Home Companion* gave me hope. He had a way of putting a ribbon on even the most mundane, finding the poetry in the simple incidents of daily life. Consider this passage from his book *Leaving Home*:

> For our sake, to accommodate squeamishness, Aunt Flo tried to give up butchering and be content with store-bought chicken, but it was against her principles. She cooks to bring happiness, it is part of her ministry, so to put tasteless chicken on the table is to preach false doctrine.

Doing something as ordinary as cooking chicken for the family is a very sacred thing! A profound truth opened up to me—the ordinary IS extraordinary! This is what Saint Teresa of Calcutta meant when she famously said, "Not all of us can do great things, but we can do small things with great love."

Unknowingly, Keillor, a Lutheran, taught me what the great

Catholic theologian Karl Rahner described this way: "To be human is to be divine, and to be divine is to be human." Life is a miracle; love is extraordinary. So to simply live a loving life is a miraculous and extraordinary thing, indeed. To clean the snow out of an elderly neighbor's driveway—ordinary *and* extraordinary. To sit around the table and play cards with friends or family—ordinary *and* extraordinary. To greet the beleaguered check-out person with an appreciative smile—ordinary *and* extraordinary. The difference is never in the magnitude of the action; it's in the magnitude of the heart.

If we're waiting for something great to happen, for the heavens to open up and shine light upon a gilded highway, we're missing the joyful heaven of the present moment, the infinite love available to each of us right here, right now, in the marvelous ordinariness of the everyday.

Love Is Peanut Butter

Michelle informed me, using compelling and irrefutable evidence, that I have not always been a perfect husband. I was as shocked by this as you are. After all, I shower daily and I turn the television volume down whenever she asks. I even take the garbage out sometimes simply because I notice it's starting to stink—by myself, before she even tells me. What more could she want? My first response was to assume she was joking. Big mistake. She wasn't. My next response was to be defensive and argumentative, which I quickly realized was actually proving her point. My third response was to challenge her expectations. What kind of impossible standards does this woman have?! Finally, I listened. Then I listened without interrupting.

As one of her examples—remarkably, she had more than one—she pointed to the five years when I was in formation to become a deacon. Our kids were young when I started. Jacob was eleven, Alex was six, and Adam was just three years old. I was spending three out of every four Saturdays in class, while working more than a full-time job, which included some travel. Also, I was volunteering at the parish and teaching a confirmation class, coaching two youth soccer teams my kids played on, and in the midst of all this chaos we started StreetLights Outreach. Every moment of my scant free time was spent reading, studying for exams, and writing papers. During this period of our marriage, Michelle pointed out, I was not the best husband. I withheld emotional support, companionship, and even some joy. I wasn't proud of this, and I joked a little only to diffuse the sting and embarrassment. In defense of my consistency, Michelle will agree that my imperfections have not been confined to these five years.

We had this conversation on a Sunday evening while Michelle was preparing school lunches for the boys. She layered peanut butter thick on a piece of bread and said, "See this? This is love. It's thick and rich, filled with flavor and nourishment. You take that same amount of peanut butter and scrape a little bit of it across forty pieces of bread. Everyone gets a sniff, but no one really gets much of anything." Point made.

Sometimes when we focus so much on what we're doing and what we're giving, we overlook what we're withholding. I was so focused on giving myself over to my formation, my faith, my job, my community, and my kids, that I was withholding my presence, my companionship, and my joy. I had made love safe by sharing myself more widely rather than more deeply.

When Jesus observed the poor widow giving from her need while the wealthy gave from their want, he was condemning an unjust and exploitative system. I needed to come to terms with the reality that I had created and perpetuated a parallel system of sorts within my own marriage. The currency in question was far more valuable than dollars and cents; it was the currency of time and attention, the very presence and essence of myself. Michelle was giving her all to our home, our family, and our relationship; I was giving my leftovers and withholding the balance of my heart and soul.

We tend to address the call to be generous, especially the call to be generous with the self, from a perspective of what we're giving. Perhaps we can gain a different perspective by asking what we're withholding. Indeed, what part of our love and mercy do we withhold from the world and why? I guess we have to each answer that for ourselves—how much do I hold back and why? This requires a sincere in-depth self-examination.

Do I spread the peanut butter thick and rich? Or do I merely scrape a little across the surface? Do I share my compassion deeply or just broadly? Sure, I love my family and friends, but who doesn't? As for the stranger in our midst, an unborn child who hasn't been named, the refugee fleeing violence, the cranky neighbor who complains about everyone and everything, the coworker who once stabbed me in the back... sometimes I protect my insecurities and vulnerabilities more than I share love and compassion, so I leave a lot of love in the jar.

Ultimately, thanks to the wisdom of Michelle, I have learned that we can go through all the motions, do all the right things, and end up with a whole lot of nothing. Love spread thin like watery peanut butter lacks flavor and texture. But love that's thick, rich, and layered deeply, the kind of love that leaves our jars empty, offers the nourishment our world—and our marriages—so desperately needs.

Wonder
and Awe

Delighting in Fat Rabbits

On Easter Monday, I wiped chocolate from my eyes and headed to the gym. I had to work off about five pounds of PEEPS and jellybeans. What twisted irony is this, anyway? *Jesus is risen from the dead?! WOW! Let's celebrate by self-inducing a diabetic coma!* PEEPS, by the way, is a registered trademark of Peeps & Company and in no way is responsible for my Easter gluttony.

On the way out the door, I checked the temperature. Fourteen degrees. My first thought was... in April? So I checked again. Still fourteen degrees. My second thought was less shock and more color, but not the uplifting color of new life found on eggs cradled in Easter baskets. Not at all. This color was of a much darker hue. If profanity is indeed the highest form of poetry, then I became Shakespeare. Fourteen degrees inspired a vulgar sonnet so emotive it would have left pirates red-faced.

How quickly the joy of Easter slips through our fingers! It was 5:40 a.m. on the morning after Easter Sunday and I was cinching a saddle on a horse named Bitterness. Why? Because the temperature was colder than I would have liked? How utterly pathetic. In raising my sons, I constantly reminded them to be judicious with their anger, to channel the power of anger toward big issues that matter, such as the kidnapping of girls by Boko Haram or the rapid melting of arctic ice. Yet there I was, hypocritically cursing the weather like Don Quixote flailing at windmills. What is parenting if not an endless minefield of your own hypocrisy?

As a life mantra, I have adopted a simple phrase: *Life is a joy- ride.* I tell myself to drink daily from the stream of gratitude and splash the waters of joy on my face. It's how I would like to live, but it's not always how I choose to live. Too easily I allow the world to affect my mood rather than self-directing my disposition to positively affect the world. Easter calls us to spread that joy across humanity. Yes, sometimes it's colder than we would like. And sometimes the Packers lose. And sometimes the rabbits eat our geraniums. But none of that matters. What does matter is the journey and, with the proper disposition, the ability to appreciate a cold morning, enjoy the game regardless of the outcome, and delight in fat rabbits.

You might be familiar with this quote by Maria Robinson: "Nobody can go back and start a new beginning, but anyone can start today and make a new ending." Perhaps that's ultimately the attitude to which Easter calls us. Regardless of what has happened in our lives up to this moment, we still have hope for the rest of our lives here on earth and beyond. We can write a new ending to our story. As long as I have a joyful attitude, I can have a joyful journey.

One can criticize me, I suppose, for reducing resurrection to a bumper sticker. We're talking about the single greatest reality-changing event in history, and here I am turning it to a margin doodle in a middle school cheerleader's notebook: *a joyful attitude makes for a joyful journey*. A bit obvious, isn't it? If you want to call it history's greatest understatement, I won't argue. You might be right. But I'm reminded of the Jesuit ripple philosophy on education. The Jesuits do not measure the success of their universities by the performance of their students. Instead, they measure success based on how people who meet their graduates are affected. In other words, they expect a Jesuit education to have a ripple effect in the world. A joyful disposition generates the ripple effect of the resurrection. It's a two-step process. First, be joyful. Second, infect the people you meet with your joy.

Oliver or Brian?

Oliver leaned on his cane with both hands and surveyed the scene. "This is good," he said. "What you guys is doin' here is good." Assuming the role of elder statesman in the Whitney Park neighborhood, Oliver's calming presence far out-measured his slight frame. He continued his public pondering, "It's good to see all the kids from this neighborhood playing out here together. I'm glad their mamas brought 'em. Kids playin' on the playground, mamas sittin' and talkin'. Some of these kids, their mamas didn't bring 'em, but their daddies did. It's really good to see the daddies watchin' the kids."

About two hundred and fifty people had gathered for one of our StreetLights Outreach Block Parties. Maybe more. The oldest sat on scooters, the youngest in strollers. Black, white, and brown with all shades in between, they came from diverse histories to this shared time and place. Some were homeless, a few were gentrified professionals, and nearly half were kids, although it was impossible to count as they darted, dodged, and weaved between parents, picnic tables, and trees. Everyone seemed to be smiling.

It was difficult for me to converse with Oliver. Lord knows I tried. He was a fascinating man and I wanted to hear more of his story, more of his experiences coming of age in Chicago's Cabrini Green. He spoke in generalities, always linking it to the moment, "I seen some bad stuff. Real bad. But that's why I'm here now. I gots to make sure my grandbabies stay outta trouble, you see. An' these other kids, too. I gots to be lookin' out for them 'cause ain't no one lookin' out for the kids where I come from." The struggle in communicating with Oliver was not in his willingness to share or my willingness to listen; it was in all the interruptions. Everyone wanted to say hey and engage Oliver's warmth. He knew all their names, where they lived, and what they had going on in their lives. It was a privilege to stand in his glow and witness the stream of exchanges.

Oliver had moved into the Whitney Park neighborhood sometime over the winter. In just a few short months, he had adopted a six-block area and all the families who lived there. He wasn't waiting for social workers, government programs, or public funding. Oliver was simply taking it upon himself to do what he could to create a safe and supportive neighborhood for families in this fragile part of the city.

About an hour later I found myself talking to another man, Brian, on the fringe of the gathered crowd. Standing a good six-and-a-half feet tall, Brian looked down on the scene before him and wondered what it was all about. He had been walking past the park, noticed the crowd, and wandered over to see what was going on. Brian was urgent about making two things clear to me: he didn't live in this neighborhood and he was a Christian. Brushing aside my invitation to grab a burger and join the picnic, Brian remarked that nothing meaningful was going on here. "Look at these people," he said. "They're not really building community. You want to believe they are, but they're just sitting and talking with the people they already know." Of course, Brian saw only the moment before him. He had no idea that not long ago these same people stayed locked in their houses and apartments, afraid of one another.

I invited Brian to join me as I continued walking from table to table, from small group to small group, making idle talk, spreading cheer, sharing stories. He declined. Before he left, however, he did accept my offer of a cookie for the road.

As I reflected on the evening later, these two men stood out. Oliver never once mentioned his faith or his religion. He never spoke of being a Christian, nor did he have to. His actions said everything. Brian, however, spoke of being a Christian within the first two minutes of our meeting. I wouldn't have known if he hadn't told me.

Jesus Wears Socks with Birkenstocks

The door sprang open and a man splashed through. Courtney and Cassi pretended to ignore him, but couldn't when he loudly called out, "HELLO, DUDE-ETTES!" Being the only patrons in the coffee shop, they smiled and nodded politely. Cassi turned to Courtney and mouthed, "Wow."

Everything about this guy looked like a haphazard, last-minute Easter basket. He was wearing green plaid shorts, a vibrant orange Hawaiian shirt, pink socks hiked to his knees, and heavily worn Birkenstock sandals. The ensemble took courage for a lot of reasons, including the weather. He had great hair, however—both women acknowledged that—which flowed as though it belonged on the cover of a grocery store romance novel.

The barista emerged and the women turned back to each other, but their attention remained at the counter where the conversation was one-sided with high volume.

"HI, MITCH. IS YOUR NAME MITCH? YOUR NAME-TAG SAYS MITCH."

"Yes, I'm Mitch. What can I get..."

"HI, MITCH! I'M JOSH. CAN I GET A LARGE DARK

CHOCOLATE MOCHA, PLEEEASE?"

"Coming right up. Anything else?"

"YES, PLEASE, A BLUEBERRY SCONE. A BLUEBERRY SCONE AND A AND A AND A DARK CHOCOLATE MOCHA, PLEASE. A LARGE DARK CHOCOLATE MOCHA, PLEASE—FOR JOSH. MY NAME IS JOSH."

Then things got quiet. Mitch got busy, Josh stood silently with his hands folded, and Courtney and Cassi returned to a conversation about garden statues of meditating frogs. After Easter brunch with their parents earlier, the women had activated their tradition of "running away." It was a game resurrected from childhood when they hid in their shared bedroom closet and pigged out on Easter candy. Now in their late thirties, they escaped to Cafémmaus, a coffeeshop a few blocks from their parents' house, where they indulged in double caramel lattes instead of chocolate eggs.

Life had gotten crazy, so time together without interruptions was rare and treasured. They left their husbands, kids, and phones with Grandma and Grandpa while they ran away for a couple of hours. It was a win/win/win arrangement. No one complained.

Their conversation had been meandering naturally, as one would expect of sisters close in age, effortlessly flowing from child-rearing and schools to fashion and religion. Prior to Josh's story-worthy entrance, Mitch-the-barista had disappeared and they sat alone, the shop's only customers on this sunny but windy afternoon. They had been laughing freely at memories of childhood mischief, recalling the time they cut their father's hair while he napped, and Cassi had guffawed a loud snort, causing Courtney to tear-up with laughter.

That was the moment when Josh burst into their lives.

Having received his mocha and scone, Josh welcomed himself to a table right next to them, a bold violation of the social buffer in the otherwise empty café. The women angled their shoulders away and continued their conversation.

"Why is it so empty in here?" Josh asked. He was oblivious, but at least more softly spoken than earlier. When the women didn't answer, he leaned in and asked again, "Why are you the only people here?"

Courtney interrupted her own sentence to retort somewhat abruptly, "Probably because it's Easter Sunday. People are spending the day with family." She emphasized *family* in a not-so-subtle hint that Josh was not part of theirs.

"So why are you here?" Josh asked. "Don't you have families? I don't have a family. My parents died and I have one sister but she lives in Portland, Oregon, on the west coast. Her name is Miriam."

Cassi reached out and touched Courtney's forearm. It was such a simple gesture from the younger sister but changed the tenor of the moment. Courtney breathed deeply and was brought back from the world she wanted to the world she was in. Stress, it has been said, is what happens when we wish things were other than they are. Courtney felt herself relax into presence. She adjusted her posture and opened to Josh, "It must be hard to be alone."

Josh smiled and divided his blueberry scone into thirds, handing a piece to each of the women. "My dad always told me that you're never alone when you share what you have."

First World Problems

The on-screen program guide on my television stopped working. This was annoying in a way that exposed me as utterly sad and pathetic. Rarely do I sit down and disconnect from the world, so when I do, I feel entitled to complete mindlessness. Now, I realize you're tempted to judge me here, and I suppose that's fair. Sloth is one of the deadly sins after all. When I sin, I tend to do so in a way that is sad and pathetic as opposed to wild and exciting, which, sadly and pathetically, would sell a lot more books. Stories about lust and wrath have far more commercial value than stories about sloth.

Without a program guide, American television is mostly a giant digital hairball of mind-numbing sludge with an occasional MASH rerun peppered in, the proverbial golden needle in the haystack of bad reality shows and home shopping networks. Arghh! How would I find *Star Trek: The Next Generation* among the rubble of obscure cable networks?

Sitting feet-up in my recliner and clicking through the endless channels, I grunted something under my breath about the Neanderthals who run the cable company. Michelle looked up from her book, obviously annoyed, and offered a solution, "Why don't you open the app on your iPad and use the program guide that's online?" Any person who is reading a book while another is watching TV automatically adopts the self-satisfying smugness of someone who is aware that humanity would be better served if they were in charge. They're usually not wrong about that.

"My iPad is way upstairs," I said.

"Well, my goodness," she clucked like a schoolmarm with a moral superiority complex, "aren't you just heavily burdened with first world problems? It's a good thing there's a rear camera in your truck so you don't have to, you know, turn your precious head." That's her way of saying she loves me. I'm a lucky man.

I tend to appreciate sarcasm only when it's my own. She was right, of course, and I knew it. I have the privilege of living in a world where we drink hot coffee—which someone else brews and pours—while watching a movie in the bright sun above the clouds. And we do this while homeless children dig through dumpsters in the cities we fly over. I am not at all proud of this, and I am embarrassed at how quickly I can slip from gratitude.

We live a long way from that manger in Bethlehem where there was no television. Or coffee. Or indoor plumbing. Perhaps the distance erodes our perspective and, with it, our gratitude. Increasingly, it feels like at least 80 percent of everything we hear and read in a day is negative. We seem to have perfected the art of criticizing, condemning, and complaining. No matter how incredible and amazing life is, we find things to gripe about. This is not how Christian people with Christian hearts ought to respond. Is it? I don't think so. Heck, it's not how any decent human being with a beating heart ought to respond.

Our ancient stories offer a timeless recipe for happiness through the examples of the shepherds and the Blessed Mother. The shepherds respond to a newborn infant with gobsmacked amazement. They cannot wait to post the news on Facebook and Instagram. Think about that. The gift of life, the gift of divine love living among us and within us is a miracle far more inspiring than anything that'll turn up in your Google search. Everything else is so ridiculously trivial by comparison. Yet do we have the shepherd's good sense to respond with joyful awe?

And Mary—you have to love this girl. If anyone has something to complain about, it's Mary. Having this child wasn't her idea.

She didn't ask to travel to Bethlehem and give birth among the animals in the middle of the night. And then all this unexpected, uninvited company dropped in. And you realize shepherds weren't well-known for their manners and hygiene. They elbowed their way in and crowded around with bad breath, severe body odor, and all sorts of gaseous emissions. So what does Mary do? Our Scriptures say she reflected on all this in her heart (Lk 2:19).

Wow. Can I learn from that! There is so much upside to simply taking in the world around us and reflecting on what an unbelievable miracle it all is. Such contemplative awareness of and reflection on the present moment is a powerful form of prayer. We can gain so much perspective, appreciation, and gratitude. Instead, we surround ourselves with so much noise and expectation.

Perhaps the most effective solution to all our first world problems—traffic congestion, slow internet speeds, bad calls by home-plate umpires, and just about everything else that frustrates us—is to place ourselves inside that manger outside of Bethlehem.

Jeremiah

A scrawny wisp of a ten-year-old boy came wheeling up to our StreetLights Outreach Block Party on a bicycle with only one pedal. He would push down as hard as he could with his right foot, trying to create enough momentum to crank the pedal 360 degrees, and then sort of push along with his left foot. His name was Jeremiah, and I swore that if you stacked the letters of his name on edge, they'd be taller than he was. At first he was a little shy, refusing the hamburger I offered because he didn't have any money. But once I told him the burgers were free, he gladly devoured one, and then another. And another. This little kid pounded away six hamburgers, several mountains of potato chips, and I have no idea how many cookies. Then he shoved a handful of cookies into the pockets of his sweatshirt and said he was going to go tell his brothers and sisters to come over to the park and get something to eat because, he said, "we never eat like this at home."

"You never get hamburgers at home?" I asked mostly as a form of active listening. I knew how it was for many of the kids in this neighborhood. They ate breakfast and lunch at school, and dinner was a bit of a crapshoot. But this was July. There was no school.

"No," he said. That wasn't what he meant, so he clarified, "We never get to eat until we're not hungry anymore."

Go ahead and let that steep in your tea for a moment.

Most of us have the privilege of eating until we're full, and many of us keep expanding that capacity. We even joke about it as we age, patting our increased girth with self-deprecating pride. But standing before me in the wealthiest nation in human history was a kid who wasn't talking about eating until he's full. He was talking about never being able to eat until the hunger went away. This is what I do between meals! I snack to make the hunger go away. Could it be, I wondered, that I snack as much or even more than Jeremiah and his siblings eat all day?

While all this was going on, a couple of our Spokes of Hope volunteers fixed his bike and gave it a second pedal. As he rode off, Jeremiah was an entirely transformed kid, exploding with hope, excitement, and unquenchable energy. When he returned about twenty minutes later, he had four sisters and two brothers with him; all were wide-eyed. Then he raced off again to tell some friends and cousins.

In the meantime, his mother showed up to check it out. Her presence anchored the children, and they swarmed our serving lines like a hive of bees with its queen. When we were done for the evening, we packed up all the leftover hamburgers, hotdogs, buns, chips, cookies, and sodas, and we gave it all to her. As her caravan of kids left the park, each loaded with a bag or box full of food, she could be heard saying over and over, "Praise Jesus, praise Jesus, praise Jesus," as tears rolled down her cheeks.

For me, this was a resurrection moment. You see, when the Romans crucified Jesus, they didn't just want to kill him; they wanted to kill his entire message and his movement. They wanted to kill hope. To preserve their own power and privilege, they wanted to kill his ideas about human value and dignity. They saw these as dangerous notions. So when Jesus rises from the dead, the entire body of his work, his teaching, rises with him. Love of God and love of neighbor rises to new life. Matthew 25—what you do for the least, you do for me—rises from the tomb. The beatitudes—blessed are the poor in spirit—the compassion of the good Samaritan, the dignity of the leper, the forgiveness and mercy revealed in the parable of the prodigal son, the value of the woman at the well, and the hope of the centurion whose servant was ill...it all rises to new life, the exact same new life expressed by the woman and her children in the park. Praise Jesus.

Two thousand year later, we're still living out that resurrection. Every time we spread love into the world, every time we feed the hungry, comfort the sick, welcome the stranger, we are giving flesh, blood, and breath to the living Christ. We aren't just celebrating resurrection; we BECOME resurrection. And that should fill us with joy until we're stuffed full, with enough extra to shove it in our pockets to carry to others.

Let's Put an End to This

I finished writing this book during the Great Covidian Dystopia of 2020. Weird times. Worse than the virus, though, was the way we managed to politicize a pandemic. How does that work? Seriously, what has to happen for human beings to turn a global health crisis into a political argument? I'm still confused by that. From now on, whenever I read the Exodus stories about the plagues in Egypt, I'll be wondering if there was a constituency of folks hitting up Twitter with claims that the frogs and locusts weren't real. No doubt there would have been plague deniers.

Adam Savage from the show *Mythbusters* famously said, "I reject your reality and substitute my own." The humor is in the ludicrousness of the statement. How can we willy-nilly swap out reality for a different version that fits our personal ego-narrative better? Yet, we do it all the time. Much of objective reality has been supplanted by whatever tapestry each person weaves in order to validate his or her preexisting perspective. Arguably, the result has been a disaster to our social fabric, the earth's climate, the integrity of democracy, human equality, and Christianity as well as religions of all stripes. But, you might argue, that's merely my version of reality. Fair enough.

Love, I hope we all agree, is real. We might have differences about where love comes from or how it should or shouldn't be shared, but hopefully we can all agree that love is real. Likewise, I think we would all agree that hate is real. Again, we might have different perspectives on the origins of hate, but I think we will agree that it is real. Very real. Too real. We've all seen and experienced too much hatred to seriously deny that it is real.

As we navigate the traffic circles, potholes, and detours along life's journey, we each have to make choices about which way to steer. Unfortunately, we seem to assume we have only two options: left or right. However, as noted, these choices often represent skewed realities. What if we approach every issue, every decision, every crisis with a different set of choices: love and hate? Reality. What if we simply choose the most loving path in every situation? Yes, that has the potential to be risky. Hate has a devious way of making us feel safe about ourselves, and love demands we accept constant vulnerability and occasional self-sacrifice. But isn't the reality of love worth the risk? I guess I'd rather err on the side of love than on the side of hate. I pray you would, too. Peace.

PS. I contracted the COVID-19 virus about three weeks before this manuscript was due to the publisher. Being prone to self-delusion and deception, I thought I would be Superman and fight through it. I'd keep working. Wow, was I an idiot! I got so very sick. I ended up over a month behind on my deadline, so I want to extend sincere thanks to everyone at Twenty-Third Publications for their kindness, patience, support, and prayers.